Valuing Banks in Uncertain Times

with special attention to Islamic Banks

Published October 2009 by

Spiramus Press Ltd
102 Blandford Street
London W1U 8AG
Telephone +44 20 7224 0080

www.spiramus.com

ISBN 978 1904905 82 0

British Library Cataloguing-in-Publication Data.

A catalogue record for this book is available from the British Library.

Printed in Great Britain by the MPG Books Group, Bodmin and King's Lynn

To family and close friends – so all important

En speciaal voor Pap en Mam een dikke knuffel voor hun nooit aflatende steun, enthousiasme en trots.

Acknowledgments

When I finished my research into the use of Residual Income models to estimate the value of banks, I did not plan to ever publish it beyond my thesis. One publication on the subject was certainly more than enough. But after yet another mention of "excluding financial institutions" in relation to share price estimation I eventually concluded that maybe it would be a good idea to publish this for a wider audience after all.

All errors are, of course, my own, but I would not have been able to get all the other parts right without some help. My sincere thanks go to Prof Simon Archer for his invaluable support during my research, his proof reading effort and for doing the honours of writing the foreword. Equally thanks go to Professor Rifaat Abdel Karim who was the co-supervisor for my PhD research.

To my dear friend Dr Julinda Nuri for her valuable input and support. Further thanks go to Peter Goodman for his random thoughts (as one does) on Value at Risk and to Alison Swaisland for her assistance with obtaining the forecast data.

Finally to all my friends and family for their support in which ever shape or form. To anyone I may have forgotten to mention rest assured that your contribution was equally well valued.

About the author

Dr Natalie Schoon, CFA first came across Islamic finance while living and working in the Middle East and decided to embark on a research project to see how these banks would compare with conventional financial institutions when it comes to the estimation of their fundamental value. It was only after she started that she realised that all previous research done on the topic of valuation specifically excludes financial institution. The original research which is underpinning this book covers the period 1993 – 2002 and was the basis for Natalie's PhD thesis. In order to address how well the model holds up in an economic crisis, the sample period has been extended to include the period 2003 – 2008, which has lead to some interesting findings.

Natalie has worked in international financial organisations such as ABN Amro, Gulf International Bank and Barclays Capital before joining an Islamic bank based in the city of London in 2007. She began her career in Islamic Finance whilst working in Bahrain, Kuwait and Dubai during the late 1990's. Natalie is an accredited trainer for the Islamic Finance Qualification and can be contacted at mail@formabb.co.uk.

Foreword

To produce a book on valuing banks in the 'uncertain times' of 2009 is an ambitious venture, but one for which Natalie Schoon, a CFA charterholder whose doctoral thesis dealt with the valuation of banks, is well qualified. She succeeds in showing, in this book, that fundamental analysis using a model based on residual income and analysts' consensus forecasts is able to indicate whether the market valuations of a large sample of banks are above or below estimated fundamental values and, perhaps more significantly, that the 'overvaluations' and 'undervaluations' follow the economic cycle. While this finding may seem entirely intuitive, it flies in the face of the semi-strong form of the Efficient Markets Hypothesis (EMH) – as normally interpreted - which has had such a dominant place in the finance literature. While fundamental analysts have always made it their business to detect variations from the EMH, and confidence in the EMH has undoubtedly waned considerably *ex post* in the light of the financial crisis which burst out in 2008, the overvaluation of bank shares, and the probable gross overvaluation of some, could have been detected *ex ante* using the model developed and applied by Dr Schoon.

She also shows how the model may in principle be applied to Islamic banks, in spite of their differences from conventional banks, although a lack of data makes such an application problematic in practice.

Dr Schoon's work, as presented in this book, is a most interesting and valuable development of the work, on estimating fundamental values, of scholars such as Steven Penman, Thomas Copeland, James Ohlson, Richard Frankel and Charles Lee, none of whom developed and applied a model specifically for conventional banks, let alone Islamic banks. I therefore commend her book as a major contribution to financial analysis, which loses nothing through being very readable. As an accountant, I find it gratifying to see a demonstration that financial accounting data, in combination with other data in the public domain, can yield such useful estimates of 'fundamental value'. Financial accounting data is expected to serve a variety of purposes, and financial accounting rules are subject to controversies such as those over 'fair value'. For the financial analyst, financial accounting reports are not finished, but semi-finished, products which require a further stage of processing for decision purposes. This book shows how such a further stage of processing can yield powerful results in bank valuation.

Professor Simon Archer
ICMA Centre, Henley Business School
University of Reading
September 2009

Contents

Table of Figures and Tables

Why Value?

The Industrial Revolution, globalisation and the segregation of ownership and control have all significantly strengthened the requirement to be able to put a value to a business. The question "Why Value?" is therefore not one that has only recently surfaced. The requirement to measure current and future (expected) profitability is a concept that has mainly developed over the last 250 years or so, but has been debated over the centuries, particularly in combination with the concepts of risk and return. As early as 1776 Adam Smith stated that:

> "The owner [of the capital], though discharged of all the labour, expects that his profits should bear a regular proportion to his capital. [...] The lowest rate of profit must be more than sufficient to compensate the losses to which the employment of stock is exposed. The lowest rate of interest must more than compensate the occasional losses to which lending is exposed." Adam Smith[1]

Smith clearly identified not only the need to measure profitability, but also recognised that risk and return are linked to one another in such a way that higher risks need to be offset by higher returns.

The ability to value a business will assist shareholders in their capacity as its owners in their investment decision-making process. In addition, being able to put a value to a business is equally relevant to other stakeholders with an interest in the business such as employees, governments, regulators and suppliers.

The research study that forms the basis for this book shows that, over the period of the study, in excess of 80% of the share price of banks is explained by its fundamental value. Although what drives the other

---

1 Smith, A. (1881) *An Inquiry into the Nature and Causes of the Wealth of Nations, Abridged version with notes and appendices by Wolsely P. Emerton, M.A. B.C.L.*, Oxford: James Thornton

20% is not clearly defined, it is at least in part associated with market sentiment and herd behaviour among investors. The market turmoil that started off with the subprime debacle in the United States mid 2007 has had a significant impact on the economy, with banks being taken over and/or nationalised, and a significant drop in the value of all the major exchanges. As a result of large write downs, the resulting lack of liquidity in the market and, equally important, the loss of trust in the banking system, have drastically reduced lending practices which in turn has had a knock-on effect throughout the global economy. At the time of writing, we still have to see what the impact of the various rescue packages will be and how rapidly the economy will recover, and comparisons with the Great Depression of the late 1920s, early 1930s have already been made.

The current downturn begs the question whether the sharp decline in share prices implies that the value of the underlying companies has changed dramatically in a short space of time. Or is price maybe not the best benchmark to determine company value, given that price includes some type of psychological element? The answer probably lies somewhere in the middle and is unlikely to be easy, and although there are likely to be more questions than answers, interesting enough to pay at least some attention to.

We will start with a brief review of the theoretical framework surrounding the valuation of companies, and which model appears to be most suitable for firm valuation. The question that then arises is how banks differ and the impact of these exact differences on the valuation model. Is it possible to use the same model and value a bank? As will be shown, it is indeed possible although the components of the models will have to be determined carefully.

Islamic banks have additional challenges attached to them when it comes to valuation, such as the fact that transactions have to be based on an underlying asset or an enterprise. Valuation of Islamic banks is currently further hindered by, among others, a lack of data, relatively small bank size and the fact that they are mainly based in countries that are still classified as emerging markets. On the other hand, this does not mean they cannot be valued in a similar way. On the contrary, it is possible, albeit more challenging. A number of the issues facing Islamic bank valuation, however, are similar to newly started banks in similar jurisdictions.

The data used for the study that forms the basis of this book predates the global financial crisis of 2007/2008. Although current events do not by definition invalidate the results, they do raise a number of related questions such as how the model presented might hold up throughout an economic cycle and whether or not the asset bubble and subsequent bust could have been predicted.

The remainder of this book is divided into two main sections. The first part explores different types of valuation models and how the selected "residual income model" can be applied to the valuation of banks as well as to Islamic banks. The second part will focus on challenges which are not necessarily only applicable to banks and will consider issues such as the impact of the media on share prices, valuation in uncertain times and market sentiment.

Part 1 – Valuing Banks

1 Valuation of Firms

Ever since Adam Smith's Wealth of Nations, the desire to be able to measure current and estimated future profitability of a firm, both in isolation and in comparison to others operating in the same market segment, has intensified. In 1890, Alfred Marshall stated in volume 1 of the Principles of Economics[2]:

> "What remains of his capital at the current rate may be called his Earnings of Undertaking or Management."

Marshall's 'Earnings of Undertaking' are in fact identical to Economic Profit, which is calculated by subtracting a capital charge from net income after taxes. The 'Earnings of Undertaking' are based on current returns, and do not necessarily include future expected growth or the risk related to the (long-term) investment. Expected future growth and risk are, however, important issues for consideration. Any highly profitable investment is typically linked to a higher risk for the investor. Risk and future growth are further intertwined with current and future expected returns, capital and cost of capital.

1.1 Valuation Components

Regardless of which valuation model is used, the underlying components – risk, expected growth, estimated future returns, capital and cost of capital – will, in some shape or form, have to be incorporated. The estimation of each of these parameters is briefly described in the remainder of this section.

---

2 Marshall, A. (1895) *Principles of Economics*, 3rd Edition, London: Macmillan & Co page 157

1.1.1 Growth

Growth most importantly concerns the growth that can be sustained by a firm over longer periods of time, typically for at least the next three to five years. In its most simplistic form, the sustainable growth rate can be determined by multiplying the earnings retention rate (which represents the proportion of income the firm retains for re-investment in the company) by the return on equity (ROE)[3]. The underlying assumptions when determining the growth rate are that a firm wants to grow as fast as possible, there is no requirement to issue new equity, and the firm wants to maintain its current capital structure and dividend policies. This raises an interesting issue during the current financial crisis, where particularly banks are receiving additional capital injections from their respective governments. This will be addressed in more detail in part 2, chapter 7 which reviews the potential impact of financial crises on valuation.

The main issue related to the determination of growth remains that the growth rate is generally based on historic data. However, history does not necessarily repeat itself.

1.1.2 Risk

In general, it can be stated that the return on an investment should reflect the level of risk incurred. In other words, an investor will only be willing to invest in a higher risk asset if he will have a reasonable chance to receive a higher return reflecting this. The risk-return trade off in combination with his individual risk profile is one of the main motivators behind the investor's decision, at least, to consider an investment. The frontier on which, in equilibrium, all optimum, diversified portfolios are positioned is known as the Capital Market Line

---

[3] The sustainable growth rate is typically calculated as follows: $g^* = (R)(ROE)$ where g^* represents sustainable growth, R is the Retention Ratio and ROE is the Return on Equity

(CML) which is devised by Markowitz[4]. He developed the Expected Return – Variance (E-V) hypothesis based on the rules that an investor:

1. Maximises discounted expected, or anticipated returns; and

2. Considers expected return desirable and variance of return undesirable.

The CML represents the rates of return on efficient portfolios with different risk levels. It takes into account that an investor will always have some investment in the risk-free asset in his portfolio to mitigate some of the potential risk he takes which other investments. Whether or not an investment suits an individual investor will depend on his risk appetite and his optimum portfolio as measured by the CML.

1.1.3 Returns

> "Economists and accountants differ on the proper definition of profit. To the accountant, profit is the excess of revenues over expenses and taxes and is best measured by earnings. To the economist, earnings fail to include an important expense item, the opportunity cost of equity capital, contributed by the shareholders." Kimball[5]

This statement neatly defines why returns are difficult to measure – how to define a return depends very much on whom one is discussing the subject matter with.

Returns are, however, a major component in a valuation framework, and both current and future (expected) earnings need to be defined carefully. Different schools of thought exist when it comes to the identification of returns, the main ones being earnings, free cash flow

---

4 Markowitz, H. (1952) *Portfolio Selection*, The Journal of Finance, 12(1), 77-91

5 Kimball, R.C. (1998) *Economic Profit and Performance Measurement in Banking*, Boston: New England Economic Review, July/August, 35-53

and dividends, each with their own advantages and limitations.

The main limitations of earnings are associated with the use of realisation and matching principles in accounting which results in recognition of earnings in different periods than the underlying cash receipts and disbursements. Free cash flow, which addresses this issue, has its own disadvantages and neither free cash flow nor earnings incorporates how changes in future business conditions are expected to affect them. Dividends reflect the return to shareholders but do not represent the overall returns of the company. Although it could be argued that dividends are the only relevant valuation attribute since, ultimately, only payoffs count and dividends alone can be consumed, they have two main drawbacks. First, dividends paid reduce the actual market value of the company by the equivalent of the dividend payment, which can be observed as soon as a stock goes ex-dividend. Secondly, dividends have a negative impact on earnings in subsequent periods, mainly because the firm cannot reinvest dividends paid.

After all is said and done, earnings appear to be a superior measure when it comes to valuation, a standpoint which is neatly summarised below:

> "Even though accountants have not formally recognised the goal of having an earnings figure that measures value, they have done a remarkably good job of achieving this goal. That's the magic in earnings."
> Black[6]

This is further based on Black's findings that the Price/Earnings multiple is more stable than the Price-to-Book Value ratios, which leads to the conclusion that earnings as they are reported in the financial statements can be used directly when determining the value of a company.

---

[6] Black, F. (1980) *The Magic in Earnings, Economic Earnings versus Accounting Earnings,* Financial Analysts Journal, 36 (November/December), 19-24

The expected future value, which is discounted in the value of the company, can for exactly the same reason be based on the reported earnings figures, and the value of a firm can be defined as the current book value plus an infinite sum of discounted residual income or earnings over and above the required return on equity.

In order to predict estimated future returns with any degree of accuracy, the following key issues will need to be incorporated in the analysis[7]:

- **Micro-economics of the firm.**

  In general, structural Residual Income models have not attempted to identify the main type of micro-economic shocks that impact residual income. Specifically, no reference is made to the distinction between demand and supply conditions, shocks that are specific to the individual accounting entity, and shocks that affect the entire industry.

- **Competitive Forces**

  Competitive interaction of the firm with firms in the same industry needs to be incorporated in the assessment of residual income since competitive forces eventually drive residual income towards a long run equilibrium level of zero. As a result of the working of competitive forces, the consensus among researchers and practitioners is that the rate of mean revision is around 38% per year, meaning that any exceptional returns due to a competitive advantage will on average only last for a period of around three years. As a result, the majority view is that expected future returns should be determined using a two-stage approach. During the first stage of around three years, the growth rate of return is determined based on the expected growth of the individual firm. The second

---

7 Walker, M. (1997) *Clean Surplus Accounting Models and Market-based Accounting Research: A Review,* Accounting and Business Research, 27(4), 341-355

stage provides the terminal value, which attempts to capture the reversion of the firm's long-term returns to the industry average.

1.1.4 Capital

A firm's capital base consists of the total capital available to the firm to apply to the business and to generate a return. For any type of organisation, the total capital base consists of the following:

- Equity Capital which includes share capital and reserves;
- Long-term Debt such as long term loans and bonds issued;
- Short-term Debt such as short term working capital loans, bank overdrafts and revolving credits.

When applying the Miller Modigliani Theorem[8] it would not make a difference to the firm on whether it finances itself with debt or equity. However, due to taxation, cost and leverage issues, firms typically make a calculated choice on how to structure their finances.

1.1.5 Cost of Capital

The cost of capital is generally defined as the opportunity cost of capital for the firm's existing assets[9]. In order to estimate the cost of capital,

---

8 Miller and Modigliani (1961) showed that in perfect and complete capital markets, a firm's dividend policy does not affect its value. The basic premise of their argument is that firm value is determined by choosing optimal investments. The net payout is the difference between earnings and investment, and is simply a residual. Because the net payout comprises dividends and share issues/repurchases, a firm can adjust its dividends to any level with an offsetting change in shares outstanding. From the perspective of the investors, dividend policy is irrelevant, because any desired stream of payments can be replicated by appropriate purchases and sales of equity. Thus, investors will not pay a premium for any particular dividend policy. (Constantinides, G.M., Harris, M, Stulz, R.M, *Handbook of the Economics of Finance: Corporate Finance*, Amsterdam: Elsevier B.V.

9 Brealey, R.A., S.C. Myers and A.J. Marcus (2003) *Fundamentals of Corporate*

the different components of capital need to be considered. Owing to the fact that equity and debt capital have different characteristics, each demands a different required return. When making investment decisions, the firm will normally base itself on the total available capital, and not make the distinction between debt and equity components. Cost of capital is commonly expressed as the Weighted Average Cost of Capital (WACC) in equation (1), which provides an approximation of the total cost of capital.

$$WACC = r_{Capital} = r_{Debt}\left(\frac{D}{(D+E)}\right) + r_{Equity}\left(\frac{E}{(D+E)}\right)$$

Equation 1 – Weighted Average Cost of Capital

where *r*: Required return (on capital, debt or equity)

E: Market value of Equity

D: Market value of Debt

In order to enable international comparison, the cost of debt should be calculated on an after tax basis, which results in the effective cost of debt being calculated as r_{debt}(1-tax rate).

Whilst the market value of equity of a listed company can be determined relatively easily based on the share price quoted in the financial markets, the perceived market value of unlisted debt might be more difficult to determine. Bond prices quoted in the financial markets for a company with the same characteristics and credit worthiness could be used as a bench mark or alternatively, the book value of debt can provide a reasonable approximation of the value of the debt. The interest rate of fixed-rate debt can then be used as an approximation for the required return on debt.

Finance, International Edition, New York: McGraw-Hill, p 321

The cost of both debt and equity is not only based on market conditions, but also on the perceived risk of the investment. Hence, if WACC is estimated correctly, it can be used as an appropriate risk adjusted discount factor. For banks however, capital mainly consists of equity without any significant debt (see section 2.2.2). As a result, only the required return on equity is relevant to determine a bank's cost of capital.

1.2 The Models

There are two basic ways to look at the value of a business:

- Value created over a specific period of time. This consists of earnings (including dividends) over and above the cost of capital employed during the reporting period. This information is available in the company's periodic reporting and includes how the income is distributed.
- Value of a company at a particular point in time. This is a function of its current and future expected earnings, rate of return, capital and cost of capital. Where future expected earnings are concerned, the most important characteristic is whether they can be sustained and grow in combination with the risk taken to obtain them.

For a company that is not a going concern but likely to be terminated within a short period, the emphasis will be on the value created during the current period. For any going concern, both the value created during the current accounting period as well as the value at a particular point in time are relevant for the investment decision making process. It is the value of a company at a particular point in time which is the main subject of this book. Although many different models have been applied to the valuation of companies, some are ultimately more suitable than others for many different reasons. The main criteria used here are the ease of use with publically available information, the number of variables and, as far as possible, proven reliability. The most significant different models are detailed further in the remainder of this chapter.

1.2.1 Discounted Cash Flow

Discounted Cash Flow (DCF) models determine the value of a company as the present value of all expected future cash distributions discounted at the opportunity cost of capital. The general arguments in favour of these models are that they are best positioned to value a company since the value of the company's equity, assuming the business is a going concern, arises from the company's capacity to generate cash flows for the equity shareholders.

Two main types of DCF model can be distinguished, the Dividend Growth Model (DGM) and the Free Cash Flow Model (FCF), which are both based on the discounting of an expected future cash flow at the required return.

Dividend Growth Model

The Dividend Growth model (DGM) uses the level of dividend, expected growth in dividends, and an appropriate discount rate to determine the value of the business, where generally explicit forecasts of dividend are used for the short-term forecasting period in combination with a Continuing Value for the going concern as represented in equation (2) below:

$$P_0 = \frac{Div_1}{(1+r)} + \frac{Div_2}{(1+r)^2} + \dots + \frac{Div_t}{(1+r)^t} + \frac{Div_{t+1}}{(r-g)(1+r)^t}$$

Equation 2 – Dividend Growth Model

where P_0: Price at time 0

Div: Dividend

r: Required return

g: Growth

The value of the firm is then calculated as the price (P_0) times the number of shares. The main disadvantage of this model is that it mainly considers the pay-out to equity investors and does not necessarily incorporate any future additional returns which may be achieved by reinvesting the profits in the firm and will potentially be foregone by paying out dividends.

Free Cash Flow Model

This model is similar to the DGM represented in equation (2), but replaces the expected future dividend stream with the expected free cash flows to the firm, which are in turn discounted at the appropriate discount rate. Free cash flow represents the cash that a company is able to generate after laying out the funds required to maintain or expand its asset base. Free cash flows can be calculated as follows:

	Net Income
+	Amortisation/Depreciation
-	Changes in Working Capital
-	Capital Expenditures
=	**Free Cash Flow**

The main question arising in the context of Discounted Cash Flow models is which cash flow series (dividends or free cash flow) best represents the expected future earnings stream and thus the value of the firm. In all fairness neither incorporates how changes in future business conditions are expected to affect the future cash distributions and, in addition, the DGM does not take into consideration the advantages of retained earnings as a basis for growth.

Regardless of whether dividends or free cash flows are used, the main driver of these models is that the expected value of the firm is arrived at by discounting the expected cash flows at a benchmark which is represented by the firm's cost of capital.

1.2.2 Economic Profit

The main characteristic of Economic Profit models is that they calculate a periodic spread between the Rate of Return on Capital and the Cost of Capital. A variety of Economic Profit models exist, the main ones being Residual Income and Economic Value Added.

Residual Income Models

Residual Income in itself can be defined as earnings over and above the cost of capital, discounted at the required return on equity as detailed in equation (3)

$$RI_t = \left(Earnings_t - (r_e \times B_{i-1}^e)\right)$$

Equation 3 – Residual Income

The Residual Income valuation models[10] determine the value of a company as the value of invested capital plus the present value of the stream of differences between (accounting) earnings and a charge for the use of capital, discounted at the cost of capital, and can be defined as:

$$V_t^e = B_t^e + \sum_{i=t+1}^{\infty} \frac{E_t[RI_t]}{(1+r_e)^i}$$

---

[10] Lee, C.M.C., J. Myers and B. Swaminathan (1999) *What is the Intrinsic Value of the Dow,* The Journal of Finance, 54(5), 1693-1741

Frankel, R. and M.C. Lee (1998) *Accounting Valuation, Market Expectation, and Cross-sectional Stock Returns,* Journal of Accounting and Economics, 25, 283-319

Equation 4 – Basic Residual Income Valuation Model

Substituting Residual Income (RI) with its individual components then gives:

$$V_t^e = B_t^e + \sum_{i=t+1}^{\infty} \frac{E_t[Earnings_i - (r_e \times B_t^e)]}{(1+r_e)^i}$$

Equation 5 – Residual Income Valuation Model

Where B^e_t is book value of equity at time *t*, $E_t[..]$ is the expectation based on information available at time *t*, $Earnings_i$ are the Earnings for period *i*, B^e_i the book value of capital at the start of the period *i*, and r_e the required return on equity.

Equation (5) attempts to represent the consensus view which indicates that the value of a company is not based on a single notion of dividend, cash flows or earnings, but is a combination of current book value and future expected residual income, discounted at the cost of capital. This model is generally found to have a high predictive power, especially using longer specific forecasting periods.

Similar to The Dividend Discount models and Free Cash Flow models, the main disadvantage of the Residual Income model is related to the fact that it contains an element of expectation, which is generally classified as unobservable.

Economic Value Added

Economic Value Added (EVA) as developed and trademarked by Stern Stewart is based on the more general measure of Economic Profit, and is, in its simplest form, defined as follows:

$$EVA = (r - c^*) \times Capital$$

Equation 6 – Economic Value Added

where *r* represents the rate of return, and c^* the Weighted Average

Cost of Capital.

EVA is based on the Residual Income model, where operating profits are reduced by a charge related to the use of capital. In further development of EVA, Stern Stewart identifies a total of 164 adjustments that are required in order to 'correctly' estimate net operating profits and capital. The underlying reason for these adjustments is to compensate for what Stewart identifies as shortcomings in the accounting approach. Although Stewart's objective is to create a superior valuation measure, it results in an unmanageable model since the data required is often not directly available on the balance sheet, income statement, or notes. Although some marginal evidence is found that EVA's amendments might be incrementally important, the difference does not appear to be economically significant, may suffer from size-bias, and that even adjusted for size, they do not adjust for events outside the control of management such as general market movements. In addition, there is hardly any evidence that suggests that companies with a high EVA outperform the market.

1.2.3 Which Model?

Identifying the most superior valuation model is complicated, mainly due to the fact that each of the individual models has its own advantages and disadvantages attached to it. Ultimately, it is generally accepted that if applied correctly, each of the models will provide exactly the same equity valuation Even so, most research in the general area of valuation of a firm concludes that Residual Income model (also often referred to as economic profit model), the oldest and both, in theory and practice, the most tested type of model, still continues to provide the most accurate results when determining the value of a business. With the main advantages being that they can easily be applied using accounting data, require estimates for a smaller number of variables, and provide a better valuation measure than the others. This further enhances the practical use of the Residual Income model as a tool for financial analysis.

The main issues that will need to be addressed with the Residual Income model are:

1. **Forecasting the infinite time horizon**

   The Residual Income model asks for an infinite time horizon for forecasted earnings. However, earnings are considered to be mean reverting as a result of competitive forces, and to revert to zero after around three years, thus reducing the need to forecast specifically for a longer time period.

   The Continuing Value starts at the end of the finite, three year, forecasting period and is discounted back to time t=0, and can in its simplest form be represented as follows:

$$\frac{CV}{(1+r_e)^i}$$

   Equation 7 – Discounted Continuing Value

   It is calculated for the going concern using the long-term expected growth rate as represented in the equation (8):

$$CV = \frac{RI_3 \times (1+g)}{(r_e - g)}$$

   Equation 8 – Continuing Value

   where g represents the expected long term growth rate.

2. **Subjective expectation**

   Forecasts may contain an unobservable element of subjective expectation. Using I/B/E/S consensus forecasts instead of individual estimates will reduce the subjective element.

Frankel and Lee[11] researched the use of the I/B/E/S consensus earnings forecasts as a proxy for market expectations of future earnings, and find that the resulting estimate of firm fundamental value has a high predictive power and reduces the subjective element of expectation.

Box 1 - Why use I/B/E/S forecasting data

Although not the only company collecting data, I/B/E/S, which is the abbreviation of Institutional Brokers' Estimated System, is well regarded among academics, researchers and practitioners alike and is deemed to provide consistent high quality earnings data. A view which is, among others, shared by William Sharpe. Not bad as far as recommendations go. Detailed and consensus estimates for up to 26 components including pro-forma EPS, revenue/sales and net income are collected for over 45,000 companies worldwide with history going back as far as 1976 for US Data and 1987 for international data. Data is provided by around 1,200 contributors. The consensus forecast is based on the consensus found between all the contributors.

[11] Frankel, R. and M.C. Lee (1998) *Accounting Valuation, Market Expectation, and Cross-sectional Stock Returns,* Journal of Accounting and Economics, 25, 283-319

The final model, including the Continuing Value component reads as follows:

$$V_t^e = B_t^e + \sum_{i=t+1}^{3} \frac{E_t[Earnings_i - (r_e \times B_t^e)]}{(1+r_e)^i} + \left(\frac{RI_3 \times (1+g) / (r_e - g)}{(1+r_e)^3} \right)$$

Equation 9 – Residual Income Valuation Model

In the model, three future earnings estimates are required beyond current earnings which, in the event of an equity valuation model as detailed in equation (9) can be determined on a per share basis. Each of the estimates can be derived using the I/B/E/S consensus Earnings per Share (EPS) and estimates for the next periods, which are labelled F1MN and F2MN. Year-end book values are dependent on the current year Return on Equity or Earnings, and a sequential process is used to estimate future values.

Box 2 – Estimating Forecasted Earnings

Forecasted Earnings per Share for the first forecasting period are computed as the year *i* consensus forecast, divided by the average book value per share during the period t-1. Use of the average book value rather than year-end reduces the chances of extreme outliers, either positive or negative.

$$\text{Forecasted earnings}_t = F1MN/[(B_{t-1} + B_{t-2})/2]$$

For the second forecasting period, the Forecasted Earnings are calculated based on the two-year consensus forecast (F2MN) in accordance with the following equation:

$$\text{Forecasted earnings}_{t+1} = F2MN/[(B_t + B_{t-1})/2]$$

For the Continuing Value component, the Forecasted Earnings are calculated based on the two-year consensus forecast (F2MN) and the long term consensus forecast (LTMN) in accordance with the following equation:

$$FROE_{t+2} = [F2MN(1 + LTMN)]/[(B_{t+1} + B_t)/2]$$

The key to ensuring that the model provides an accurate valuation of a bank lies in the correct estimation of the individual parameters.

2 Why is Bank Valuation so Difficult?

> "Banks remain among the most difficult companies to value despite the multitude of regulatory and reporting requirements imposed on them. It is hard to determine the quality of their loan portfolio, to figure out what percentage of their accounting profits results from interest-rate mismatch gains, and to understand which business units are creating or destroying value." Copeland, Koller and Murrin[12]

What is it that makes any researcher and econometrician, as well as the majority of practitioners, run a mile when it comes to valuing a bank? How come they are deemed so much more difficult to value than any other company? Is it the sheer size of some of them or does it have something to do with general understanding of the industry? Or is it maybe mainly because of the fact that, even though banks produce their annual statement of accounts in line with accounting standards and provide a significant amount of information in the body of the annual account, we are still not really clear how they make their money? Transparency (or the lack of it) when it comes to off-balance sheet instruments, combined with the fact that banks are subject to a different set of risks we may not necessarily understand and increasing complexity of some of the relatively new products do not help either.

But does this mean we should just forget about valuing banks because the task is too difficult? Granted, the mess that the industry got itself in and that unfolded at the back end of 2008 does not make attempting to value banks more attractive. On the other hand, one issue that is

[12] Copeland, T.E., T. Koller and J. Murrin (2000) *Valuation: Measuring and Managing the Value of Companies*, 3rd Edition, New York: John Wiley & Sons, 437 – 438

becoming clear from the 2008 credit crisis is that the market does not just trade on what it knows. Trading appears susceptible to herd behaviour and (over) reaction to news, both actual and expected.

The majority of market participants will agree that the ability to have a reasonable estimate of the value of any corporation is important to the working of the market, which would include the financial industry. Even though some of the parameters are estimated in a different way and a range of different types of risk need to be considered, the underlying model remains the same.

2.1 Bank Valuation Model

Valuing banks might be difficult, but is by no means impossible. Unlike other companies, banks' assets do not consist of plant, machinery or goods. In the same vein, banks' liabilities consist largely of deposits, which will need to be repaid, but are not the same as loans. Liability management, and the subsequent potential to create value, is part of the operational activities of the bank. Hence, any form of capital which is not equity, should not be considered as purely financing in the same way as debt financing is part of the funding of a company. As a result, valuation of a bank should be based on the Residual Income model for equity valuation as represented in equation (10)

$$V_t^e = B_t^e + \sum_{i=t+1}^{\infty} \frac{E_t[Earnings_i - (r_e \times B_t^e)]}{(1 + r_e)^i}$$

Equation 10 – Residual Income Valuation Model

In this model, the required return on equity capital (r_e) is assumed to remain the same for the going concern, and will not change over the lifetime of the bank. In order to overcome the issue of having to forecast for an infinite time horizon, a continuing value will be introduced after three years of specific forecasting. This captures the fact that after three years forecasting becomes increasingly difficult, the introduction of forecasting errors is likely and the long-term residual income reverts to the industry mean.

The Continuing Value will be calculated for the going concern, using the long-term expected growth rate at the end of year three:

$$V_t^e = B_t^e + \sum_{i=t+1}^{3} \frac{E_t[Earnings_i - (r_e \times B_t^e)]}{(1+r_e)^i} + \left(\frac{RI_3 \times (1+g) / (r_e - g)}{(1+r_e)^3} \right)$$

Equation 11 – Residual Income Valuation Model

The assumptions underlying this model are that systematic risk levels as well as the riskless rate of return are assumed to remain constant over time for the going concern (represented by the Continuing Value), unless significant changes are expected in the perceived risk levels of the bank. In an equity valuation model, the value can be determined on a per share basis, in which case the earnings are determined on a per share basis. The value of the bank as a whole is then equal to the value per share multiplied by the number of shares outstanding. In the event of a per share valuation, the earnings in equation (11) can be replaced by Earnings per Share.

The key to the accuracy of the model's result lies in the correct application of the individual parameters as detailed in the next section.

2.2 The Parameters

Although the model only asks for a few parameters, it is important that these are estimated correctly which will ensure that the value that is the result of the model is accurate. Each of the parameters required is detailed in this section.

2.2.1 Return

Off-balance sheet instruments such as guarantees, derivatives and letters of credit generate a significant part of the returns of banks, and the expected returns related to those as well as on-balance sheet items need to be considered when determining the total return of a bank. Although the potential liabilities associated with the off-balance sheet instruments are not typically recorded in the financial statement, the earnings reported by the bank as reported on the income statement generally include all realised and unrealised earnings, be they generated by on or off-balance sheet instruments.

In order to establish potential future returns for an individual entity, notes to the financial statements need to be analysed carefully, and competitive advantage will need to be taken into consideration when determining the sustainability of these earnings. Applying I/B/E/S consensus forecasts for the future estimated earnings ensures a rigorous analysis will already have taken place. In addition, applying a consensus forecast will reduce any subjectivity which is naturally present in estimations.

2.2.2 Capital

For any type of organisation, the total capital base consists of the following:

- Equity Capital;
- Long-term Debt;
- Short-term Debt.

Besides equity and debt, banks further have the funds of current and deposit account holders at their disposal and these are used to finance loan and investment operations. Although this implies that the bank's customers can be major liability holders, these funds are not considered part of the capital base of a bank, but should rather be viewed as what they are, the source used to fund their operations.

This also holds for venture capitalists and investment banks, where all or part of the invested funds are managed at the investor's (the client's) own risk, like discretionary portfolios and mutual fund investments. The funds are invested on behalf of the client, with the bank generating revenue from the investment service they provide. These funds are considered to be part of the liability management of the bank, but do not form part of the bank's capital base, which consists solely of equity capital. Like corporate debt, the cost of attracting deposits is based on the perceived risk a depositor is taking, which will be reflected in the overall net earnings.

A similar view can be adopted with regards to subordinated debt, with the possible exception of subordinated debt specifically issued to meet capital requirements. Subordinated debt issued as a pure source of funds can be considered as operational and hence should be excluded from capital, and the related costs will be deducted in the calculation of earnings. In contrast, subordinated debt issued to meet capital requirements could be considered for inclusion in the capital of the bank. However, the announcement by Deutsche Bank early 2009 not to refinance their subordinated debt but instead pay the higher cost to service the debt under the existing agreement, supports the conclusion that even subordinated debt issued with the intention to meet capital requirements is part of the banks operational funding. In addition, it might be difficult, if not impossible to distinguish between these types of subordinated debt. For this study subordinated debt is considered as operational and not as part of capital.

2.2.3 Cost of Capital

The ability to measure the value of a firm on a stand-alone basis provides an indication of the overall value, but remains a relative concept as long as there is no comparison to other companies in the same industry or market place. One of the main benchmarks in valuation is the cost of capital of a firm in relation to the cost of capital of the market portfolio as a whole. Because a bank's capital constitutes solely of equity, there is no requirement to determine the Weighted Average Cost of Capital. Instead, the cost of equity, which is defined by the required return on equity, suffices. The main models to determine the required return on equity, namely the Capital Asset Pricing Model (CAPM) and the Arbitrage Pricing Theory (APT) are reviewed in further detail.

2.2.3.1 Capital Asset Pricing Model

The Capital Asset Pricing Model (CAPM) is developed based on Markowitz'[13] expected return – variance (E-V) hypothesis which is based on the rules that an investor (i) maximises discounted expected, or anticipated, returns and (ii) considers expected return desirable and variance of return undesirable. Markowitz then identified the Capital Market Line (CML), an efficient frontier on which, in equilibrium, all optimum, diversified portfolios are positioned. CAPM is defined as a utility function of investor preferences and replaces the Capital Market Line with the Security Market Line (SML), which is a graphical representation of the CAPM benchmark. CAPM has the following underlying assumptions:

- Investors have homogenous expectations regarding the possibilities of various end-of-period values for all assets;

---

[13] Markowitz, H. (1952) Portfolio Selection, The Journal of Finance, 12(1), 77-91

- Common probability distribution describing the possible returns on the available assets is joint normal;
- Investors choose portfolios that maximise their expected end-of-period utility of wealth;
- Investors may take long or short positions of any size in any asset, including the riskless asset.

CAPM is represented in the following equation:

$$\boldsymbol{r_e = r_f + \beta(r_m - r_f)}$$

Equation 12 – Capital Asset Pricing Model

where r_e is the expected return on the security, r_f represents the risk-free rate represented by Treasury Bills or other government paper, r_m is the market rate of return and β (beta) indicates the systematic, undiversifiable risk of the investment in comparison with the market. It measures the correlation between an investment's value and movements in the overall market applying the following equation:

$$\beta_j = \frac{\delta_j}{\delta_m}\left(Corr(j,m)\right)$$

Equation 13 – The Calculation of β

In equation 13, j represents the return on an individual equity with m representing the return on the overall market. The resulting β defines the standard deviation of an individual asset relative to the standard deviation of the market, multiplied by the correlation co-efficient between the return on the risky asset *j* and the market *m*. For the market as a whole, β equals 1.0.

A high β implies that the stock price is more volatile than the average market, i.e. it goes up more than the average market price when prices are going up and goes down more than the average market price when the average prices are going down. A low β implies that the stock price is relatively unaffected by swings in the overall market.

2.2.3.2 Arbitrage Pricing Theory

The Arbitrage Pricing Theory (APT) is a multifactor asset-pricing model which expands CAPM with additional factors and measures the sensitivity of an asset's returns to each additional factor with an individual factor-β. APT is based on the notion that besides the riskless rate and the systematic risk determined by CAPM, there is more than one other factor that systematically affects the returns of the market or an individual equity.

A variety of different additional factors can be considered for inclusion such as company size, book-to-market value and a company specific risk premium. The main issue with a multifactor asset-pricing model is which factors to incorporate, and which factors to ignore. It is possible to incorporate factors that do not have any inherent explanatory value themselves, but are included solely due to the fact that they fit the data presented. Furthermore, there is a risk that an additional factor added to the model may adversely affect the explanatory value of other factors.

The following factors are most generally used in the APT:

1. Industrial production index;
2. Short term real rate;
3. Short term inflation;
4. Long term inflation;
5. Default risk.

With the resulting model being:

$$r_e = r_f + \beta_1\big(r(f)_1 - r_f\big) + \beta_2\big(r(f)_2 - r_f\big) + \ldots + \beta_n\big(r(f)_n - r_f\big)$$

Equation 14 – Arbitrage Pricing Theory

where $r(f)_n$ represents the expected rate of return on the market portfolio in relation to the nth factor, which is independent of all other factors, and β_n represents the sensitivity of the stock return to this factor.

Although there is some evidence that additional factors are relevant in the calculation of the cost of capital, it is generally found that this is not significant and certainly not off-set by the effort of collecting the additional information or the potential risk of introducing additional forecasting errors. Multifactor models may lead researchers to search the data for variables that describe the cross-section of average returns with hindsight and have no predictive power (i.e. data mining or data snooping).

2.2.3.3 CAPM or APT?

Rejection or acceptance of both CAPM and APT are never clean, and there is always a possibility that rejection of CAPM is due to an incorrect proxy for the market portfolio and the resulting poor estimates of the market. Company size and book-to-market value of equity appear to have some explanatory power over and above the market, which provides a reason to suggest that the multifactor asset-pricing model is better situated to provide a benchmark than CAPM.

Even though both CAPM and APT have disadvantages, they are still the most widely accepted models to determine the risk level of an asset or company in relation to the overall market portfolio. The relative simplicity of CAPM, in relation with the fact that incorrect choices of factors may easily invalidate the APT, make CAPM the most useful model to determine the required return on equity.

2.2.4 Risk

Banks are subject to risks different from other types of firms as a direct result of the type of business they are in (see table 1). Some of these risks equally exist in other types of firms such as business and liquidity risk, whereas others such as market and interest rate risk are specific to banks. In order to quantify these risks, banks apply a measure known as Value at Risk (VaR) which attempts to measure the downside risk in one single number, taking into account financial leverage and diversification effects. The result of the VaR equation represents the maximum amount a bank is likely to stand to lose on a given day or over a number of days generally with a confidence interval of 95 or 99%. From a bank valuation perspective, any risk taken by the bank will have to be evaluated against the risk management framework in place and the cost of the measures.

Type of Risk	Description
Liquidity Risk	The risk of insufficient liquidity for normal operating requirements also defined as the ability of the bank to meet its liabilities when they fall due.
Interest Rate Risk	The risk arising from interest rate mismatches in volume, maturity and type (fixed vs. floating) of interest-sensitive assets, liabilities and off-balance sheet items.
Credit Risk	The risk that an asset or a loan becomes irrecoverable in the case of outright default, or the risk of delay in the servicing of the loan.
Settlement or counterparty Risk	The risk that occurs if one party to a transaction pays funds or delivers assets prior to receiving its own funds or assets, hence exposing it to a potential loss.
Price Risk	The risk that the market price of an instrument traded in a well-defined market will be volatile. Market risk occurs in relation to debt securities, derivatives, equity derivatives and currency transactions held by a bank.
Leverage Risk (Capital Adequacy)	The risk related to the extent to which the assets of a bank may decline before the positions of its depositors and other creditors are jeopardised.
Event or Operational Risk	The risk of certain events occurring, e.g. disaster, regulatory or political events, or the (temporary) unavailability of IT systems.
Business Risk	The risks related to products, macro-economic cycles and technology changes.

Table 1 – Types of Risks for Banks

2.3 The Proof

The value of any company, banks and non-banks alike, is the cumulative result of its financial performance, and the question that remains is whether or not the model actually works with real data. Residual Income models have two different functions, to evaluate periodic performance and to determine the value of a company at a certain point in time, and it is the second purpose that is tested here. The model itself has been tested extensively on a variety of industries, but always excluding financial institutions. In order to determine whether the results are valid, they will have to be tested against a benchmark. Frankel and Lee[14] have found that the V^e_t estimates of this model using I/B/E/S consensus forecasts are highly correlated with stock prices, which will be used as the benchmark here to show whether the model works.

The assumptions underlying the model are that systematic risk levels as well as the riskless rate of return are assumed to remain constant over time for the going concern (represented by the Continuing Value), unless significant changes are expected in the perceived risk levels of the bank. As a result, the forecast earnings are estimated based on the I/B/E/S consensus forecasts as defined in section 1.2.3.

The remaining of this section details at a high level the data, statistical methods and results of the research. The detail displayed here is deliberately kept at a reasonably high level in order to ensure that a wider audience can be reached. Full details of the research including the definition of the hypothesis, full statistical methods and results of the various analyses are available from

---

[14] Frankel, R. and M.C. Lee (1998) *Accounting Valuation, Market Expectation, and Cross-sectional Stock Returns*, Journal of Accounting and Economics, 25, 283-319

http://www.spiramus.com/bank_valuation.htm

2.3.1 Data

Although Residual Income models have been empirically tested for non-financial institutions, this has not yet been done for banks. The Residual Income model for conventional banks represented in equation (15) which is repeated below is used to determine the value of a bank at a specific period in time.

$$V_t^e = B_t^e + \sum_{i=t+1}^{3} \frac{E_t[Earnings_i - (r_e \times B_t^e)]}{(1+r_e)^i} + \left(\frac{RI_3 \times (1+g) \Big/ (r_e - g)}{(1+r_e)^3} \right)$$

Equation 15 – Residual Income Valuation Model

The model consists of four parameters for which estimations are required, being the book value of equity at time *t* (B^c_t), earnings, cost of capital (r_e), and the long-term growth rate (g). Capital is a function of the model and is equal to the book value of equity at the end of the year preceding the current forecasting period.

The current Book Value of equity is represented by the book value of owners' equity, as reported on the balance sheet, with the other parameters determined as defined in section 2.2. The data for the research underpinning this section is obtained from Datastream and spans the period 1991 to 2002.

The total available sample is used in two ways and consists of banks listed on stock exchanges in markets that are considered information efficient such as *EURONEXT*, *LSE*, and *NYSE*. The dataset for this study is constructed based on the following criteria:

1. A minimum of five and a maximum of ten years of historical data are available for each of the banks in the population.

2. Only those institutions that have a listing for their banking activities are included. Combined bank and insurance companies that have a single listing covering both banking and insurance activities are excluded from the dataset.

3. All observations are taken at the same annual interval to facilitate panel data analysis.

4. Only banks located in the United States of America and Western Europe are included in the sample. Banks in Japan are not included since no financial data for Japanese banks were available in Datastream.

In order to determine how the model best captures the market-based returns, an estimation sample and a control sample are constructed. The sample provides a realistic representation of the conventional banking universe, and the bias to a particular geographical area or size is minimised.

From the original 1,718 banks in the sample, mainly for banks outside the US, the required data from Datastream (e.g. prices, financial information) are not available or incomplete. As a result, the remaining number of banks in the sample is 194, with a total number of observations of 1,677. Banks that are part of the total population are, for instance, HSBC, ABN AMRO Bank, Citigroup, Deutsche Bank, Bank of America, and Barclays. All data including the I/B/E/S consensus forecasts for each of the elements in the sample are obtained from Datastream on a per share basis. Due to the fact that the book value and price *per share* are used, any merger or acquisition activity in the period should not have a significant impact either on the value, or on the regression itself. Although this may vary from bank to bank, the total effect is deemed to cancel out over time, and the development of price and calculated value are considered to follow the same pattern. For any banks that have gone through a merger and/or acquisition, no data are available from Datastream for the original underlying entities.

Royal Bank of Scotland for example, took over National Westminster in 2000. This can be seen from the development of both the price and the value estimation, as reproduced in table 2 below (Total assets in USD millions, both estimated value and year-end price are represented per share):

Item	1998	1999	2000	2001	2002
Total Assets	129,721	139,958	462,039	521,810	648,548
Estimated Value	4.79	6.50	10.96	17.00	14.79
Year-end Price	15.28	16.04	23.71	24.06	23.47

Table 2 – Example: Royal Bank of Scotland

Both price and estimated value develop in the same way, and the data are included in the sample unadjusted, specifically since total assets and capital have developed along similar lines. This may, however, result in more extreme residual values in the regression model.

From the data items contained in Datastream, those listed in table 3 below have been used to calculate the value of a bank:

Data Item	Description
190	Dividend per share. Used to determine plough-back rate and the related effect on the future book values.
305	Equity Capital and Reserves. Used in combination with number of shares (NOSH) to determine Book value per share in the event item 1308 is not available.
625	Earned for ordinary. Net profit arrived at after deducting tax, minority interest and preference dividends, but before any reported extraordinary items and allocation to reserves.
1308	Book value per share
NOSH	Number of shares
F1MN	I/B/E/S consensus growth forecast, 1 year forward. Earnings per share
F2MN	I/B/E/S consensus growth forecast, 2 years forward
LTMN	I/B/E/S consensus long-term growth expectation. If not available, the value calculated in $FROE_{t+1}$ is used to proxy for $FROE_{t+2}$
392	Total Assets
Beta	Annual average of monthly Betas provided by Datastream. The monthly Betas are based on daily data.
Risk-free rate (R_f)	Where available government bond rates as available from Datastream are used. In all other cases, Worldscope MSCI data is used, which is only available from 1995 onwards.
Market rate (R_m)	Market rates are obtained from Datastream, calculated as the difference between time t and time t-1. The main index in a country is used as the basis to determine R_m
Price	The market price at fiscal year-end.

Table 3 – Datastream Data Items

All amounts are in USD *per share*, which are automatically provided by Datastream. The exchange rates used are those at the time of the observation.

With the exception of Price, the data elements mentioned in table 3 are used to determine V^e_t using equation (15) for which both time series analysis and cross sectional analysis were applied using panel data, with a desired confidence level of 95%.

2.3.2 Statistical Method

Without going into too much detail, the data for the 194 banks was analysed using two sub-sets of data, randomly generated from the original sample, which contained an equal number of observations. A sample regression function[15] was used in which the independent variable is the equity value of the firm calculated using the Residual Income model and there is only one dependent variable being the total market capitalisation of the bank (i.e. price multiplied by the number of shares). The values resulting from the Residual Income model in itself should be sufficient to explain the cross-sectional variations in total market value, and hence no additional explanatory variables, such as firm size, are included. The Sample Regression Function is determined using the Ordinary Least Squares (OLS) method. The OLS is a technique used to define the best fit of the Sample Regression Function in such a way that the sum of the sample residuals is as small as possible. The data is analysed using time series and cross-sectional analysis.

Data varies from sample to sample and as a result, estimates will change. It is therefore required to be able to measure the 'reliability' or

---

[15] The Sample Regression Function (SRF) is determined based on the Population Regression Function which is defined as $Y = \beta_1 + \beta_2 X + \mu$ where X is the independent or explanatory variable representing V^e_t, and Y is the dependent variable represented by the total market value, which equals the market price multiplied by the number of shares

precision of the estimate. The precision of the regression model is determined by what is known as its standard error (s_e), with the goodness of fit being determined by R^2. R^2 measures the proportion of the total variation in the dependent variable (Y) explained by the regression model.

2.3.3 Sample Details

Based on the criteria detailed in section 2.3.1, the total number of banks in the sample is 194 with a sufficient number of data points. Any bank with less than five years of calculated values has been excluded from the sample to enhance the accuracy of the results of the statistical tests. The resulting sample consists of banks from the United States and Western Europe, with in excess of 60% of the banks being based in the US (see box 3).

Box 3 – Geographical distribution of the sample

Country	Banks	%
Belgium	3	1.5
Denmark	4	2.1
Finland	2	1.0
France	3	1.5
Germany	6	3.1
Greece	1	0.5
Ireland	2	1.0
Italy	10	5.2
Norway	9	4.6
Portugal	2	1.0
Spain	8	4.1
Sweden	2	1.0
Switzerland	9	4.6
Netherlands	2	1.0
UK	7	3.6
US	124	63.9

Although the sample is significantly smaller than the total population, its geographical distribution mimics the geographical distribution of the banks in the full sample which contained all banks listed on the stock exchanges in the US and Europe.

Box 4 – Amendments for missing data elements

In a few instances not all data was available. Any amendments have been made in line with other research in the general area of equity valuation as follows:

- Where earnings are negative, 1% of total assets is used as a proxy. This percentage is determined based on the average earnings of banks over the period of this study.
- Where book value per share is not provided by Datastream, it is calculated by dividing equity capital and reserves by the number of shares.
- Where the consensus forecast for the long-term growth rate is not available, $FROE_{t+1}$ is used as a proxy for $FROE_{t+2}$.
- Observations for which no Market and/or Risk-free rate of return is available have been removed.
- Observations for which no Beta is available for individual banks have been removed.

As a result of the fact that data are no longer maintained for banks that have been are merged or have gone out of business, the sample suffers from what is known as survivorship bias[16]. Unfortunately, there is not much that can be done about this since data are often no longer available from an easily accessible source.

[16] The tendency for failed companies to be excluded from performance studies due to the fact that they no longer exist. Survivorship bias causes the results of some studies to skew higher because only companies which were successful enough to survive until the end of the period are included. Similarly, mutual fund performance may be misleading due to survivorship bias if the fund family tends to merge or discontinue underperforming funds. (www.investorwords.com).

Besides the survivorship bias that occurs, the sample is prone to the occurrence of outliers in the analysis which is the result of the variety in balance sheet size and markets in which the banks operate (e.g. national versus internationally active). This is a common problem when applying cross-sectional data analysis since it deals with all members of the population at a given point in time, and all of the banks are different in size. This results in the occurrence of what is known as heteroskedasticity[17] which is controlled for using the White Heteroskedasticity Consistent Covariance.

In order to apply a time series analysis, the number of observations should be as high as possible. The dataset for the analysis applied to this research has 10 observations per bank for the following reasons:

- The impact of mergers and acquisitions in the industry is significantly larger when applying a longer period;
- The model calls for annual data, and data is not always available for periods in excess of 10 years;
- The results of the model are not only used to identify whether the model is applicable to banks in general, but also to assess whether it can be applied to Islamic banks. For Islamic banks, only a limited history is available as is described in chapter 3.

Inherent in the nature of the Residual Income models is the occurrence of first-degree serial autocorrelation, which results from the fact that the value of a bank (V^e_t) is based on the book value in the previous

---

[17] In statistics, when the standard deviations of a variable, monitored over a specific amount of time, are non-constant. Heteroskedasticity often arises in two forms, conditional and unconditional. Conditional heteroskedasticity identifies non-constant volatility when future periods of high and low volatility cannot be identified. Unconditional heteroskedasticity is used when futures periods of high and low volatility can be identified (www.investopedia.com).

period. First degree serial autocorrelation is controlled for within the sample.

2.3.4 Test Results

The different test results lead to the conclusion that the Residual Income can, to a significant degree, capture the cross-sectional differences in stock market value of conventional banks over a significant period of time. The value calculated using the Residual Income model is highly correlated to market value and as such, the Residual Income model defined in this book and which is reproduced below, can be used to estimate the value of a bank.

Analysing the data purely on a cross-sectional basis, the results on a year-to-year basis, using the Ordinary Least Squares method[18], are as represented in table 4 below:

---

[18] The Ordinary Least Squares Method defines the best fit of the regression line in such a way that the sum of the sample residuals is as small as possible. For further detail on this statistical method see:

Thomas, J.J. (1983) *An Introduction to Statistical Analysis for Economists,* London: London School of Economics Handbooks in Economic Analysis, Second edition;

Gujarati, D.N. (2002) *Basic Econometrics,* 4th Edition, New York: McGraw-Hill International Editions

Year	Observations	Goodness of fit
1993	118	91%
1994	125	98%
1995	140	98%
1996	155	98%
1997	171	95%
1998	194	95%
1999	194	90%
2000	194	89%
2001	194	96%
2002	194	84%

Table 4 – Cross-sectional Analysis Results

Although the values in the goodness of fit of the model (also known as R^2) differ between the years, these differences are not very significant and can largely be explained by market dynamics and overreaction to market shocks in the years 1999 (Asia), 2000 (Russian Rouble) and 2002 (Dot Com).

2.4 Valuing Banks – The Conclusion

> "Stock market behaviour is driven by investor sentiment as well as by clear-thinking rationality, and speculative action can drive market values away from fundamentals, and thereby away from the 'theoretically correct' estimation given by the valuation model." Barker[19]

After all is said and done, the conclusion based on the evidence presented will have to be that, as long as the parameters are estimated correctly and the right model is applied, it is ultimately possible to estimate the value of a bank in the same fashion as is done for any other type of company. Interestingly enough, the results do show that there is an impact of bubbles and the reaction of market participants to associated news which shows up as a deterioration in the goodness of fit between the price and the estimated value determined using the Residual Income model. This relationship is explored in more detail in Part 2, Chapter 6.

[19] Barker, R. (2001) *Determining Value – Valuation Models and Financial Statements,* Harlow: Pearson Education Limited, page 6

3 Valuing Islamic Banks

> "The Islamic Finance Industry is worth about $800bn globally and is growing at an annual rate of 10 – 15 per cent. The sector's dramatic growth since 2000, when it was worth $150bn, and profusion of investment products has been fuelled by an increasing desire by Muslims for investments that comply with Islamic law. Demand has also been triggered by the big increase in wealth in the Gulf, where growth has doubled since 2002 on the back of the soaring oil price."
> Financial Times, 30 May 2008

As a result of the global growth of the Islamic banking industry it becomes increasingly important to be able to estimate the value of Islamic banks in isolation as well as in comparison to other financial institutions. Although the balance sheet structure of an Islamic bank differs from a conventional bank, conventional and Islamic banks operate in the same industry and are not substantially different in their operations. The different aspects of Islamic banks will need to be considered carefully when applying the same valuation framework as identified in Chapter 1.

Having established that the Residual Income model can, to a significant degree, capture cross-sectional differences in stock market returns of conventional banks over a significant period of time, the model is applied to Islamic banks. For Islamic banks, the estimation of parameters differs from conventional banks due, in part, to the different balance sheet structure, and the lack of availability of market data. The application of the Residual Income model to Islamic banks results in the identification of a number of issues. Although indicative, this research finds that it is possible to estimate the value of Islamic banks using the same model as can be applied to conventional banks. As for conventional banks, a Residual Income model for equity valuation is applied, with a specific forecasting period of three years followed by a continuing value as represented in equation (16) below:

$$V_t^e = B_t^e + \sum_{i=t+1}^{3} \frac{E_t[Earnings_i - (r_e \times B_t^e)]}{(1+r_e)^i} + \left(\frac{RI_3 \times (1+g) / (r_e - g)}{(1+r_e)^3} \right)$$

Equation 16 – Residual Income Valuation Model

Issues specific to Islamic banks in relation to the determination of capital, cost of capital and returns and the assumptions underlying the application of the model are described in further detail in section 3.1, which also includes issues related to, among others, lack of market data, limited sample size, and the lack of implementation of uniform accounting standards.

3.1 Islamic Bank Specifics

> "Islamic banks were developed on a foundation that does not permit the separation between temporal and religious matters. That foundation requires compliance with Shari'a for all aspects of life. [...] Accordingly, Islamic banks are founded on the concept of sharing profits and losses consistent with the Islamic concept of "profit is for that who bears risk". Islamic banks reject interest as a cost for the use of money and loans as an investment vehicle."
>
> AAOIFI[20]

The source of guidance for Islamic principles is the *Sharia'a*, the ethical framework guiding human conduct of all Muslims which includes a statement that "trading is permitted and usury is forbidden". Although

---

[20] AAOIFI (2002) *Accounting, Auditing and Governance Standards for Islamic Financial Institutions*, Accounting and Auditing Organisation for Islamic Financial Institutions, Bahrain: AAOIFI, page 26

riba literally translated means usury, it is universally interpreted as interest or a pure return on money. The main reasons for the prohibition of interest are that it enables the wealthy to make money at the expense of the less wealthy without doing anything to earn that money. Hence it concentrates wealth and promotes inequality through exploitation, whereas money should not have such self-generating properties. Profit sharing, investing and trading, however, are seen as an appropriate basis for economic transactions between the supplier of capital and the entrepreneur, and are regarded as an appropriate alternative.

Because of the requirement to comply with *Sharia'a* and the resulting absence of interest, Islamic banks not only use different modes of financing, but also different means of attracting depositors. These differences are reflected in the structure of the balance sheet and need to be taken into consideration when applying a valuation model to Islamic banks.

Where conventional banks attract and place funds with a view to generate monetary profits, Islamic banks avoid interest, unnecessary uncertainty and speculation. Islamic banks mobilise funds on an interest-free basis. The Islamic bank takes on the role of a partner in the investment, rather than the less active role conventional banks take. Within the framework of *Sharia'a*, investment decisions are based on the underlying economic principles of the investment, and the involvement of the bank is therefore to a lesser extent 'at arm's length' than is the case in conventional bank, which could result in additional concerns in the context of agency theory. In *mudaraba* and *musharaka* investments Islamic banks, and therefore their investment account holders, do not just provide funds but are considered as partners in the investment project. In a *mudaraba,* which can be described as a "partnership between work and capital", the bank provides the work (i.e. identification of investment opportunities) and the client provides the capital as a sleeping partner. Where the bank acquires *musharaka* assets (i.e. invests capital in a *musharaka* partnership) the bank typically acts as a sleeping partner. This has an impact on how the bank operates, and hence on both the assets and the liabilities of the bank.

In addition to the prohibition of *riba*, *Sharia'a* also prohibits speculation and hoarding. Financial speculation is equated to gambling, and prevents Islamic banks from, among other things, taking out forward contracts even in the form of a hedge, although there is an exception in the form of a parallel *salam* which is a forward sale contract the bank enters into to reduce its exposure to the underlying asset. One of the arguments surrounding this issue is that financial speculation leads to gains and losses without increasing the usefulness of exchanged goods, i.e. it is a zero-sum game which creates no economic value. The underlying logic related to the prohibition of hoarding is that it would result in society having fewer resources in use than there are available. Therefore hoarding deprives the needy of available assistance. In addition, it allows the hoarder to manipulate the price and create an unfair market. Other forms of price manipulation such as spreading false rumours are also forbidden within *Sharia'a.* It needs to be stated though that *Sharia'a* does not advocate equalisation of wealth, and that it does recognise that personal wealth creation is a motivating factor in the economic process. It solely requires that the wealthy circulate their wealth to increase production for others as well as themselves, and that markets and prices are fair and honest. All Islamic finance related terms used in this book are clarified in the glossary.

3.1.1 Sources of Funds

Islamic banks typically have current accounts, restricted investment accounts (RIA), unrestricted investment accounts (URIA) and equity capital and reserves as sources of funds. RIA and URIA are sometimes also referred to as profit sharing investment accounts.

- **Current Accounts.**

  Similar to current accounts of a conventional bank. Islamic banks guarantee the balances on these accounts from the equity of shareholders, but do not pay any interest or other return on their balances.

- **Investment Accounts.**

  Investment accounts are either classified as restricted (RIA) or unrestricted (URIA). The difference between RIA and URIA is that the funds of a RIA need to be invested as specified in the contract. The holder of an RIA shares in the profits and losses of these specific investments only. The bank, in its capacity as the *mudarib,* typically has no capital invested and losses are distributed between the account holders in proportion to the capital provided. In contrast, the URIA funds are applied to the liability management of the bank and the account holder shares in the profits and losses of the banks operation. In either case the holders of investment accounts bear the full risk of loss to the magnitude of their accounts if the returns on the aggregate asset portfolio investments are negative unless the bank has been guilty of misconduct or negligence. In the latter case the bank bears all losses.

  Equity of URIA is the amount remaining from the original funds received by the Islamic bank at the date of the financial statements, plus or minus their share in the profits or losses and decreased by withdrawals or transfers to other types of accounts. According to the Accounting and Auditing Organisation for Islamic Financial Institutions (AAOIFI), equity of URIA is not considered a liability for the purpose of financial accounting, because the bank is, in the case of a loss, not obliged to return the original amount of funds received from the account holders unless the bank is guilty of misconduct or negligence. As per IAS32, URIA could be classified as a "puttable instrument", a liability with equity-like characteristics.

URIA are conceptually different from accounts held with conventional banks since they share in the profit and are not paid a pre-agreed, either fixed or floating, interest rate. As a result, the participation of holders of URIA in the operational results of the bank is higher than with conventional banks, and displays more characteristics of equity. It appears to be common practice among Islamic banks to smooth the financial returns to investment accounts by varying the percentage of profit taken by the bank as the *mudarib* share, or their fee for managing the funds.

Since the introduction of the AAOIFI standard to eliminate profit smoothing, two types of reserves are introduced. The profit equalisation reserve (PER) is used to supplement the payout to URIA and shareholders dividend in years when income might be low. The investment risk return (IRR) is used to cover investment losses so that the URIA capital is effectively (part) guaranteed. Appropriations to both are at the discretion of the bank. Although the PER has both a shareholder and a URIA holder component, they do not form part of the bank's capital.

- **Equity Capital.**

  Similar to conventional banks, equity capital consists of funds raised by the bank through the sale of common shares to the public and includes any reserves attributable to shareholders accumulated by the bank over the years.

3.1.2 Sources of Income

One of the main sources of income for conventional banks is interest income, a type of income that is absent in Islamic banks. Instead, Islamic banks offer specific types of finance, for instance in the form of *murabaha* for resale of goods on credit, *istisna* for pre-finance of the production of specified items like aircraft, large equipment, or construction contracts, or *ijara* which represents a form of leasing. Although depending on the funding structure, a major source of income for Islamic banks is the management fees in the form of the *mudarib* percentage of profits of investment accounts.

3.1.3 Structure

The activities of an Islamic bank are similar to those of conventional banks, and typically comprise a combination of retail, wholesale, fund management and investment banking. However, the structure of Islamic banks is different. The relationship between shareholders and holders of RIA and URIA is governed by the *mudaraba* contract, under which one party (the *rab al mal* – the investment account holder) supplies funds to an entrepreneurial party (the *mudarib* – the Islamic bank) for investment purposes. The profit that results from operations funded by investment accounts is divided between the bank and the investment account holders according to the ratios agreed in advance in the contract. In case of a loss, the *mudarib* receives no remuneration, but does not share in the loss.

In general, the balance sheet of an Islamic bank is structured as represented in table 5 below:

Assets	
Cash and cash equivalents	
Sales Receivables	*Istisna* *Murabaha* *Salam*
Profit and Loss Sharing Investments	*Musharaka* *Mudaraba*
Leased Assets	*Ijara*
Fixed Assets	

Liabilities, unrestricted investment accounts and owners' equity	
Due to Central Banks	
Current Accounts	
Unrestricted Investment Accounts including related reserves	
Proposed Dividends	
Shareholder's Equity	Share Capital Reserves Retained Earnings

Off-Balance Sheet
Restricted Investment Accounts
Commitments and Contingent Liabilities

Table 5 – Islamic Bank Balance Sheet Structure

Furthermore the following items can be encountered:

- ***Qard***. Loan for which only the principal is repayable, used, for example, for study or marriage. On the asset side of the balance sheet, current accounts are often on the basis of *Qard*. AAOIFI suggests that, in addition, a separate statement is introduced to account for these loans as part of the financial statements;

- ***Zakat.*** Annual charitable gift applied to wealth in the form of liquid assets at the rate of 2.5% or 2.5775% of the value of assets, depending on whether the financial year is based on the lunar or the solar calendar. *Zakat* can only be used for charitable purposes.

Not only the balance sheet, but also the statement of profit and loss differs from conventional banks. In general, the statement of profit and loss of an Islamic bank contains the items represented in table 6 below:

Income	
Profit Sharing Income (Total)	*Musharaka* *Mudaraba*
Mudarib fees	
Lease Income	*Ijara*
Other Income	
Less: Income attributable to investment account holders (*Musharaka* and *Mudaraba* profit shares)	

Expenses
Operating Expenses

Net Income
Income minus Expenses

Table 6 – Islamic Bank Statement of Profit and Loss Structure

The operating expenses of Islamic banks are similar to those of conventional banks and consist of items such as personnel, premises and equipment, and depreciation. Although income attributable to investment account holders is typically reported as a deduction on the income side, some banks report this item as an expense. A few banks report excluding income attributable to investment account holders as a separate item, reporting only the net income.

In general, the financial statements of Islamic banks are much less transparent than those of conventional banks. However, the enhanced transparency of the financial statements of conventional banks is quite a recent development. In Europe, the 1989 Second Banking Coordination Directive (89/646/EEC) still allowed banks (at national discretion) to maintain hidden reserves up to a maximum of 4% of total assets. Only with the more recent introduction of more stringent accounting and reporting rules has the transparency of financial statements of conventional banks increased.

3.1.4 Financial Year

The financial year of an Islamic bank can be based either on the lunar or the solar calendar. The lunar year consists of 12 lunar months of on average 29 days, 12 hours, 44 minutes and 2.8 seconds[21]. Some of the Islamic banks use the lunar year which is around 11 days shorter than a year in the Gregorian calendar. This needs to be taken into consideration when estimating and forecasting expected future earnings and the cost of capital.

3.1.5 Accounting Standards

During its relatively short history, the Islamic financial industry has evolved, and is still evolving, towards becoming a mature industry. One of the implications of this is that, as a result of the continuing development and adaptation of accounting standards, financial statements are subject to regular changes. Although a change in accounting policy does not, in theory, have an impact on the results of the valuation model, it does increase the difficulty of applying the model. The Accounting and Auditing Organisation for Islamic Financial Institutions (AAOIFI) was established to develop a uniform set of accounting standards for Islamic financial institutions. However, during the period covered in this research, these accounting standards were

---

[21] Webster's Dictionary of the English Language (1990)

only enforced in Bahrain. In all other countries, the application of AAOIFI standards was voluntary, although recently Jordan, Sudan, and Qatar have chosen to enforce them.

3.1.6 Financial Data Availability

Historically, merchant banks were established to support national and international trade, and have over time evolved into the conventional banking industry in its current form. Although interest-free finance has long been practised in the same way as the merchant banks that were the predecessors of conventional banks, the first Islamic bank only started operations in 1975. As a result, the historic time series for Islamic banks are limited. Furthermore, although the number of Islamic banks has shown steady growth since 1975, their numbers remain low, a situation that seriously impairs the construction of a significant sample. The predictive power of the model is therefore potentially reduced; an issue that will need to be addressed by allowing for a higher number of degrees of freedom.

3.2 The Parameters

Within the Residual Income framework, dividend growth is often used as a proxy for the expected earnings growth. Islamic banks do not appear to follow a dividend growth policy. Instead, their dividend payout seems to be dependent on a number of factors, one of them being the payout to investment account holders. From an initial high-level overview of financial statements of Islamic banks, it appears that for payout to investment account holders a growth policy is often maintained, which is in general sustained out of the PER. However, in the case of overall reduced income growth, the payout to URIA may be done at the expense of the *mudarib* share and potentially the dividend payout to shareholders. As a result, the dividend payout ratio appears to be inconsistent, invalidating sustainable growth estimations for

Islamic banks based on a dividend growth assumption.

3.2.1 Return

For Islamic banks, earnings can be viewed in either one of the following ways:

1. **Income attributable to shareholders**

   This is similar to the definition of net income for conventional banks, and is defined as the income attributable to shareholders after deduction of all operational costs as well as the profit share of URIA and RIA when the gross income from their profits is included in total income. Empirical evidence exists that during the period of the study it was common practice among Islamic banks to smooth the financial returns to URIA by varying the percentage of profit taken as the *mudarib* share. As a result, the percentage of returns to shareholders may be reduced in a given period, in order to provide an acceptable return to URIA, even though the overall return on invested capital remains the same. This may be inverted in a subsequent period. In 2002, an accounting standard was issued by the AAOIFI, that attempts to create transparency in this practice by the introduction of the PER and IRR. The relative lack of transparency in the financial reporting of Islamic banks complicates the determination of net income.

2. **Income attributable to shareholders and unrestricted investment account holders.**

   In this case, the smoothing practices mentioned under the previous option will not have any influence on the value of the bank, since they do not affect the overall return on invested capital. The implication is that URIA need to be considered as equity.

3.2.2 Capital

Similar to other banks, it can be argued that capital in the form of current accounts as well as RIA should be treated as funds required to create value on the liabilities side of the balance sheet, and not as part of the capital base of the bank. URIA provide a special case. Because funds of URIA can be commingled with the bank's capital, and investments take place at the discretion of the bank, combined with the fact that the account holders share in the profit and losses of the bank, URIA have some characteristics of equity capital. On the other hand, URIA can be compared with funds related to discretionary portfolio management in conventional banks, in which case they are not considered to be part of permanent capital. This is in line with the position adopted by AAOIFI, which defines owners' equity as follows:

> "Owners' equity refers to the amount remaining at the date of the statement of financial position from the Islamic bank's assets after deducting the bank's liabilities, equity of unrestricted investment account holders and their equivalent and prohibited earnings, if any. That is why owners' equity is sometimes referred to as the owners' residual interest." [22]

Based on the above, investment accounts, whether restricted or unrestricted, would not be included in equity capital. However, the equity characteristics of URIA in combination with the fact that the bank's profit objectives are concerned with remunerating URIA as well as shareholders, warrant URIA to be included as capital in the valuation model. If the balance of URIA is included in capital, they can only be included at book value due to the fact that they are not publicly listed.

For Islamic banks, both definitions of capital have been tested in this

---

[22] AAOIFI (2002), *Accounting, Auditing and Governance Standards for Islamic Financial Institutions*, Accounting and Auditing Organisation for Islamic Financial Institutions (AAOIFI), page 32

study, in combination with the previously given definitions of earnings. The combinations that will be tested are as follows:

1. Current Book Value = Owners' equity

   Capital = Owners' equity

   Earnings = Income attributable to shareholders including Dividend.

2. Current Book Value = Owners' equity + URIA

   Capital = Owner's equity + URIA

   Earnings = Income attributable to shareholders including Dividend + Income attributable to URIA

Equity capital is determined at year *t*, but is not explicitly forecast for every following year unless significant changes in equity capital are expected besides the expected growth in retained earnings. Expected dividends are forecast for the explicit forecasting period in order to determine the value of owners' equity.

3.2.3 Cost of Capital

For Islamic banks, which do not tend to operate in efficient markets, the determination of the appropriate cost of capital is challenging. However, assuming the markets in which Islamic banks operate are weak-form efficient, it is still possible to use CAPM to determine the required return on equity and hence the cost of capital, since the required return on equity of the investor will be dependent on the perceived risk level in comparison with the overall risk levels of the market.

The cost of capital used depends on the estimation of capital. If capital was solely based on owners' equity, the cost of capital would equate to the required return on equity. However, if capital is determined to be a combination of owner's equity and URIA, the required return on capital needs to include the required return on URIA. The URIA have a different required rate of return, due to the following:

- The *mudarib* share, which is calculated as a percentage of profits on investment accounts and a major source of revenue for Islamic banks, is assumed to be equivalent to the return on URIA, and added to the return on owner's equity;
- URIA do not share in the bank's remuneration as *mudarib* for managing RIA;
- URIA are not charged with a share of directors' and external auditors' remuneration.

The cost of total equity capital to the Islamic bank is in this case determined based on the earnings before allocation between shareholders and URIA.

3.2.4 Risk

The absence of interest, and hence of interest rate risk as such, does not mean that an Islamic bank can be considered to bear lower levels of risk. Different types of risk can be identified for Islamic banks in the form of changes in asset and liability returns, and in asset values due to changing economic circumstances affecting the investments that are part of the portfolio of the bank. Although Islamic banks do not face fixed-rate interest rate risk, they do face a rate of return risk, which is similar in nature to floating-rate interest rate risk in conventional banks. Rate of return risk is mainly related to sale-based and lease instruments, and increases with longer terms. One of the risk mitigation techniques in use is to link lease rentals to a benchmark such as LIBOR or an inflation index and periodically to adjust the rental amounts.

In order to measure the risk of an Islamic bank properly, conventional bank risks need to be replaced by other risk types that cater specifically for the risks to which Islamic banks are exposed. Besides the above mentioned rate of return risk, the following two sources of risk are identified:

- **Fiduciary risk**. Risk related to the nature of the *mudaraba* contract, which places liability for losses on the *mudarib* in case of malfeasance, negligence or breach of contract on the part of the management of the *mudaraba*.
- **Displaced commercial risk.** The risk related to the common practice among Islamic banks to 'smooth' the financial returns to investment account holders by varying the percentage of profit taken as the *mudarib* share.

Although the types of risk differ between conventional and Islamic banks, the required return on equity will, in both cases, be dependent on the perceived risk levels in comparison with the risk of the overall market.

3.3 The Proof

Similar to other banks, the value of an Islamic bank is the cumulative result of its financial performance. As participants in the same industry, the model that is applied here is the same Residual Income Model for equity valuation. The assumptions underlying the model are that systematic risk levels as well as the riskless rate of return are assumed to remain constant over time for the going concern (represented by the Continuing Value), unless significant changes are expected in the perceived risk levels of the bank. Unlike other banks however, there are no forecast earnings available from the I/B/E/S consensus forecast. Future earnings are estimated based on the actual growth during the period, and extrapolated for the later periods.

The remainder of this chapter details at a high level the data, statistical methods and results of the author's research into the valuation of Islamic banks. The detail displayed here is deliberately kept at a reasonably high level in order to ensure that the findings are accessible to a wider audience. Full details of the research including the definition of the hypothesis, full statistical methods and results of the various analyses are available from http://www.spiramus.com/bank_valuation.htm

3.3.1 Data

The population of Islamic banks is significantly smaller than the 194 that formed part of the conventional bank sample. The sample consists of Islamic banks for which historical data could be obtained from the financial statements of the banks themselves.

The qualification 'information efficient' cannot be assigned to this population since these banks are, if at all public, mainly listed on stock exchanges in the Middle East and Asia Pacific regions which are at best considered to be weak-form efficient markets. Furthermore, the number of Islamic banks for which a 10 year history is available is limited, which severely influences the population size. As a result, the test results are less reliable and can only be used indicatively.

The 10 years of historical data has been obtained manually and constructed from year-end financial reports of the individual Islamic banks that are part of the sample. As for conventional banks, the interval of the individual observations is determined to be annual. However, due to the already restricted number of banks in the sample, for banks that use the lunar calendar an adjustment factor is introduced to enable comparison on an annual basis.

The data elements listed in table 7 have been manually obtained from the financial statements of the Islamic banks in the sample, and have been used to estimate the value of the Islamic banks. Unlike conventional banks, for which *per share* data are available from

Datastream, for Islamic banks dividends, book value and other data, are incorporated as a total amount.

Data Item	Description
Dividend	Dividends paid to shareholders.
Equity Capital and Reserves	Equity Capital and Reserves represents the Book value in a given year. Excludes proposed dividends. Due to the fact that URIA have characteristics of equity, the current book value of equity of Islamic banks can be represented by either the book value of owners' equity as reported on the balance sheet, or by the book value of owners' equity plus URIA. For the purpose of this study, both definitions of current book value for Islamic banks will be tested in order to determine which one provides the most appropriate valuation in combination with the appropriate definitions of capital and earnings.
Earned for ordinary	Net income after deduction of the income attributable to unrestricted investment before depreciation and taxes.
Unrestricted Investment Accounts	Balances of unrestricted investment account holders. As defined earlier, both inclusion and exclusion of this item in Equity Capital and Reserves will be tested.
Earned for unrestricted	Income attributable to unrestricted investment accounts. As defined earlier, both inclusion and exclusion of this item in net earnings will be tested.
Total Assets	Total assets as reported on the balance sheet.
Growth	Due to the absence of a dividend growth policy that can be used as a proxy for growth, the earnings growth rate is used as a proxy for sustainable growth estimations.

Table 7 – Financial Statement Data Items Islamic Banks

Market Data Availability

The most common form of testing valuation models is to compare the values determined using the Residual Income model to the market price. Islamic banks are often privately owned and not listed on any stock exchange, owing to which market data such as Beta and price are not available. Islamic banks that are publicly owned are mainly listed on stock exchanges located in the Gulf countries (e.g. Bahrain and Kuwait), and Malaysia. The majority of these markets can at best be regarded as weak-form efficient and the markets are relatively thin. As a result, the share prices are not completely reliable as a benchmark, and the Residual Income model in itself will be considered useful to determine the value of Islamic banks. In addition, the majority of the banks are incorporated in emerging markets and market rates of return and risk-free rates of return are often not available and need to be estimated.

Estimation of the Risk-free Rate of Return

Any investor would measure the expected return on investment against the risk-free rate of return also used to evaluate other investment opportunities. The nominal risk-free rate of return contains an element of inflation adjustment, which should be taken into consideration for Islamic banks as well. Risk-free rates of return for the countries in which Islamic banks are incorporated are often not available or, if they are, only for the most recent years. The economies in which most Islamic banks are based are closely linked to the US economy due to their reliance on oil revenues, and due to the fact that their exchange rates are in most cases pegged to the US dollar. As a result, in accordance with the International Fisher Effect the nominal US risk-free rate, adjusted for the inflation differential, is used as a proxy for the risk-free rate of return for the various countries. All average annual inflation rates have been obtained from the IMF World Economic Outlook.

Estimation of the Market Rate of Return

For Bahrain and Saudi Arabia, market rates of return are available from the stock exchange and the central bank respectively. For the other countries where banks included in this study are used, no official market rates of return are available, and they are in most cases based on the MSCI World Index. For two of the countries that are part of this research, Bangladesh and the UAE, neither is available. For banks based in these countries the risk premium of the countries they are economically closely related to is used.

Estimation of Beta

Beta (β) indicates the systematic, undiversifiable risk of an investment in comparison with the market. It measures the correlation between an investment's value and movements in the overall market. A high β implies that the stock price is more volatile than the average market, i.e. it goes up more than the average market price when prices are going up and goes down more than the average market price when the average prices are going down. A low β implies that the stock price is relatively unaffected by swings in the overall market. For the market as a whole, β equals 1.0.

For none of the Islamic banks either estimated or actual β is available from any data source, as a result of which a proxy is required. The general risk diversification strategy followed by most banks, would lead to the conclusion that their β would be close to 1, the overall market β. A lower β could be explained by the fact that the actual level of capital held is often higher than the minimum prescribed by the regulators. The average β of all the conventional banks that are part of this research is 0.8, but it fluctuates on a year-to-year basis, as a result of the perceived changes in risk profiles and the risk levels in comparison with the overall market.

Box 5 – Average Conventional Bank β

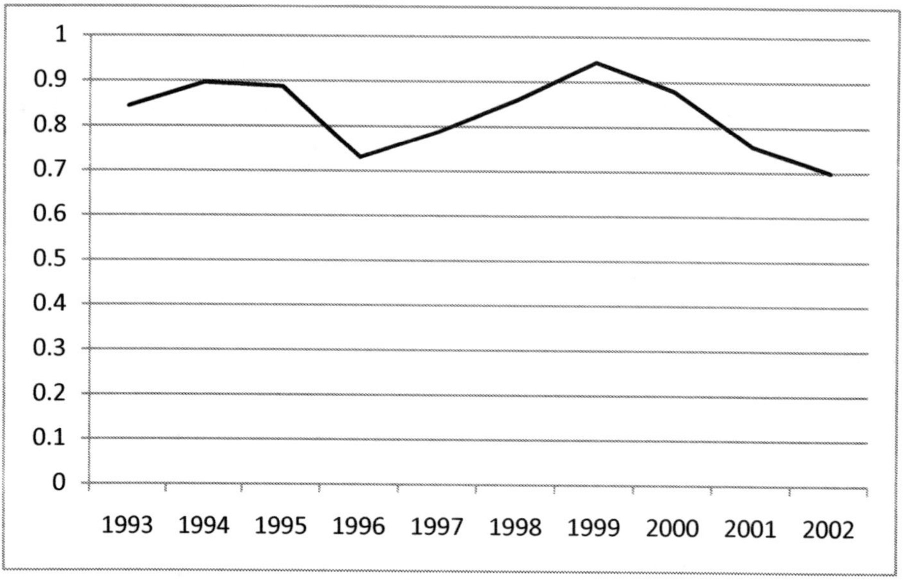

Year	1993	1994	1995	1996	1997	1998	1999	2000	2001	2002
Average β	0.843	0.896	0.887	0.730	0.788	0.859	0.943	0.879	0.757	0.699

As mentioned in section 3.2.4, in comparison with conventional banks, Islamic banks encounter different types of risk such as fiduciary risk and displaced commercial risk and they may, in addition, face a higher level of credit, market, and liquidity risks. These are related to the fact that fewer risk-hedging instruments and techniques are available, inter-bank and money markets are underdeveloped or non-existent, and there is limited availability of lender of last resort facilities. On the other hand, as a result of regulatory pressures, Islamic banks have historically been forced to hold a comparatively larger proportion of their assets in reserve accounts with central banks or in correspondent accounts, which offsets the higher risk for investors. Generally, even though Islamic banks encounter different types of risk, the risk levels of Islamic banks are no higher than risk levels of conventional banks, so that the average annual β of the conventional bank sample can be used as a proxy for β of Islamic banks.

Estimation of Growth

As a result of the relatively young history, consensus forecasts for growth for Islamic banks are not available. Using dividend growth as a proxy for sustainable growth is not feasible since Islamic banks often do not appear to follow a dividend growth policy. For the purpose of the study underpinning the findings in this book, growth for Islamic banks has been measured based on the actual growth in total distributable cash flows, which consists of total profits for unrestricted account holders and shareholders during the period with a linear trend analysis for years after the period that is covered by the data.

3.3.2 Statistical Method

As shown by the panel data and cross-sectional analysis, the majority of the cross-sectional variation in stock market prices of conventional banks can be explained by the value calculated using the Residual Income Model for equity valuation specified in equation (16). This implies that it is possible to estimate the market price based on the value calculated using the Residual Income Model. Because all conventional banks that are part of the sample are operating in efficient markets, it is possible to compare the relative value calculated using the Residual Income model with the actual market prices. This situation does not apply to Islamic banks.

Due to the limited availability, or in some cases complete absence, of data items such as the market and risk-free rates of return, as well as I/B/E/S forecast data for Islamic banks, estimations are required for some of these elements as described in section 3.3.1. However, the use of appropriately estimated proxy values should in itself not hinder the application of the Residual Income model to Islamic banks. As a result of the absence of market prices, the conventional bank test results have been used as a benchmark to determine whether or not the results for Islamic banks are acceptable.

3.3.3 Sample Details

Although the Islamic Financial industry is experiencing remarkable growth, the number of Islamic banks that are currently active is small and the number of years they have been in existence is significantly lower than the average lifespan of conventional banks. As a result, the sample of Islamic banks that was part of the study underlying this book is small. All Islamic banks in the sample are members of AAOIFI, which, due to the application of the same set of accounting regulations, enhances the standardisation of the financial statement data. Though, for the majority of the banks in the sample, the application of AAOIFI standards is on a voluntary basis. The application of different accounting standards has a negative impact on the standardisation of the financial statements, and hence the comparability of the banks in the sample. Issues that arise are, for instance, the different accounting treatment of URIA. Some banks treat URIA as off-balance sheet items, whereas others treat them as on-balance sheet instruments. In some cases, the distinction between RIA and URIA is not made at all in the financial statements. The disclosure levels between banks also differ in relation to the payout to URIA, and the profit allocation process.

The data has been manually collected from financial statements for the period 1991 – 2002 or any part since inception, and have been requested directly from the banks themselves. The total sample consists of 12 Islamic banks in different locations, with the vast majority based in Bahrain (see Box 6). For all banks that started their operations during the period 1991 – 2002, initial equity capital was reported in the first annual report, which assists in the determination of the book value of equity at the start of operations.

Box 6 - Geographical Distribution of Islamic Bank sample

Country	Banks	%
Bahrain	7	58
Bangladesh	1	8
Jordan	1	8
Malaysia	1	8
Saudi Arabia	1	8
UAE	1	8

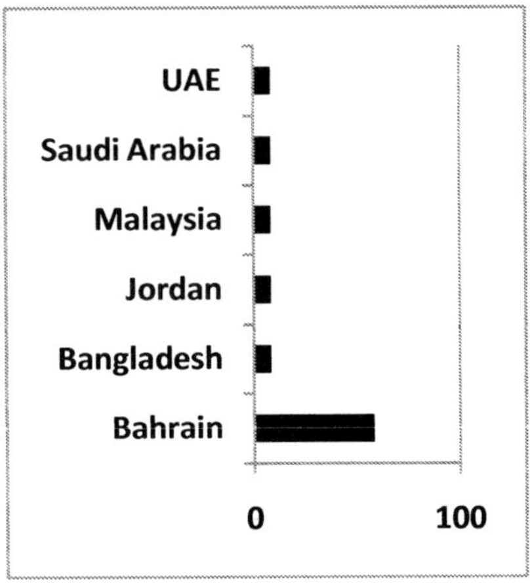

Although all the banks in the sample have voluntarily provided information, some have requested that the data be treated confidentially.

Box 7 – Amendments for missing data elements

In a few instances not all data was available. Any amendments have been made in line with the amendments made for conventional banks detailed in section 2.3.3:

- Where earnings are negative, 1% of total assets is used as a proxy. During one of the periods, two of the banks in the sample report a negative 'earned for ordinary'. One of the banks has allocated a significant amount to provisions, in the other case it was a result of impairment of fair value. For conventional banks, 6% of total assets was used as a proxy for earnings. For Islamic banks, the proxy is based on the average of 'earned for ordinary' as a percentage of total assets over the years, which is 2%.

- One of the banks initially applied the lunar calendar, but has changed to the solar calendar after the end of the financial year 1419 (corresponding with 16th April 1999). As a result, the financial year ending 31 December 2000 consists of 19.5 months. In order to enhance comparison with the other banks in the sample all years have been re-estimated at 31 December using linear interpolation.

As mentioned earlier, significant changes have taken place in the accounting policies of Islamic banks, and have continued to take place since the end of the original study. Although these do not directly have an impact on the overall reported results, URIA balances and profit allocations between RIA, URIA and the bank as a *mudarib* are not always reported and for some years have been estimated based on the notes to the financial statements.

3.3.4 Test Results

The individual components of the model (e.g. capital and return on capital) all contain some form of noise, which is caused by the use of proxies and the lack of standardisation in the annual reports. As a result of this, as well as the sample size and historic data availability, generalisations can only be made very carefully.

The challenges when valuing Islamic banks can be summarised as follows:

1. Islamic banks operate in markets that are, at best, weak-form efficient, which results in the situation that the market rate of return is less reliable. Furthermore, Beta or risk-free rates of return are often not available.
2. Not all Islamic banks in the sample are listed on a stock exchange.
3. Capital and earnings can be defined in two different ways, where the key issue is the in- or exclusion of URIA. Both situations are analysed.
4. The length of the financial year may differ in cases where the financial year is based on the lunar calendar.

Few of the Islamic banks are listed on a stock exchange, and even for those that are listed, the prices are not considered to provide an accurate representation of the value, and the market is highly illiquid.

Although the value of an individual Islamic bank differs based on whether URIA are excluded or included, the general trend in value creation remains the same. This can be observed clearly in figure 1, where for each of the banks that are part of both sample sets the value is calculated using the Residual Income model both excluding URIA and including URIA. The resulting value is then scaled by the capital to obtain the percentage return.

Figure 1 displays for each of the individual Islamic banks for which URIA data is available the value of the Islamic bank scaled for capital Excluding URIA represented by E_B** and Including URIA which is represented by I_B**. In the figure ** is replaced by the unique identifier of each of the banks in the sample.

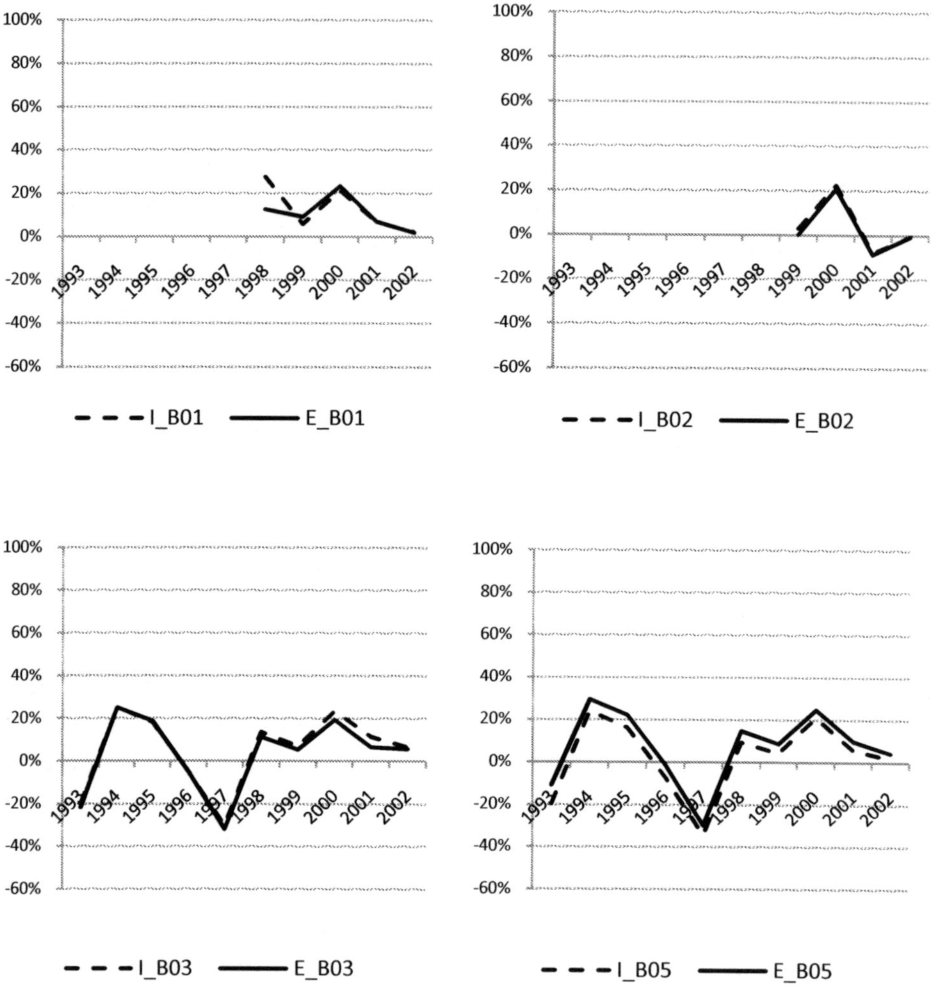

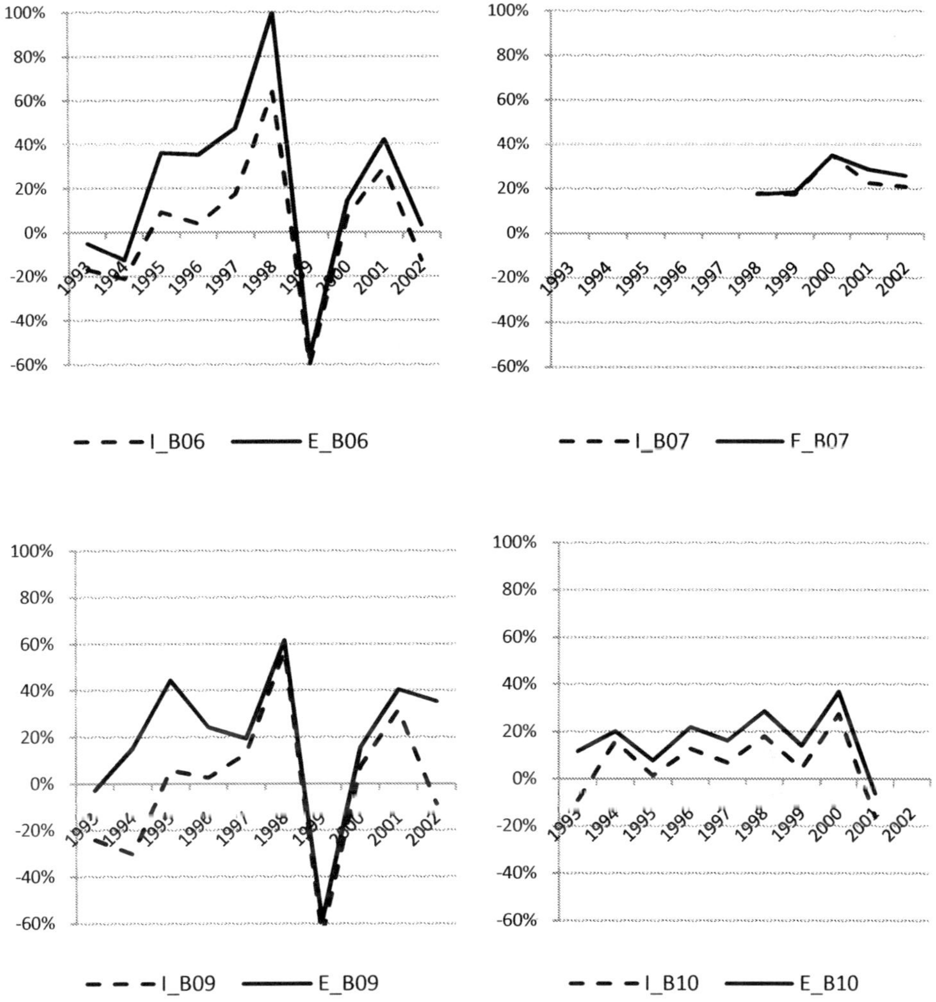

Figure 1 – Comparative Value Creation – Excluding vs Including URIA

As can be observed from the individual banks' results, the value created as a percentage of capital when including URIA is generally lower, but follows roughly the same trend as the value created as a percentage of capital excluding URIA, the difference being explained by the *mudarib* share. Due to the absence of information on withdrawals from and deposits to URIA, the results including URIA cannot be interpreted easily. Table 8 provides the percentage profit for each of the types of profit and capital combinations for each of the banks individually as well as an average:

1. Return on Equity – Net profit attributable to shareholders as a percentage of equity capital;

2. Return on URIA – Profit attributable to holders of URIA as a percentage of the total amount of URIA; and

3. Return on Total Capital – Profit attributable to shareholders + profit attributable to URIA as a percentage of total capital (equity + amount of URIA).

For the banks identified as B06 and B09, extreme changes in value are observed in 1998 and 1997 respectively. These can be explained by the fact that for these banks the market risk premium displayed a large negative movement but the results of the banks were positive compared to the previous period. From table 8, it can be observed that the returns to holders of URIA are often, but not always, less volatile than the earnings attributable to shareholders, a situation that also shows in the average returns.

		1993	1994	1995	1996	1997	1998	1999	2000	2001	2002
B01	Return on Equity						8%	9%	7%	5%	3%
B01	Return on URIA						6%	4%	6%	5%	2%
B01	Return on Total Capital						6%	5%	6%	5%	2%
B02	Return on Equity							1%	1%	1%	1%
B02	Return on URIA							3%	4%	3%	1%
B02	Return on Total Capital							1%	2%	2%	1%
B03	Return on Equity	2%	6%	8%	7%	8%	7%	7%	3%	5%	6%
B03	Return on URIA	5%	6%	7%	9%	9%	10%	11%	8%	8%	6%
B03	Return on Total Capital	4%	6%	8%	8%	9%	9%	9%	7%	7%	6%
B05	Return on Equity	10%	10%	11%	11%	10%	10%	8%	6%	6%	5%
B05	Return on URIA	3%	4%	5%	5%	5%	4%	5%	4%	3%	1%
B05	Return on Total Capital	4%	5%	5%	5%	5%	5%	5%	5%	3%	2%
B06	Return on Equity	26%	24%	36%	38%	38%	15%	16%	16%	19%	22%
B06	Return on URIA	10%	7%	6%	6%	7%	12%	5%	4%	4%	3%
B06	Return on Total Capital	14%	10%	9%	10%	11%	13%	8%	6%	6%	5%
B07	Return on Equity						13%	17%	18%	24%	23%
B07	Return on URIA						5%	6%	2%	5%	1%
B07	Return on Total Capital						13%	16%	14%	20%	16%
B09	Return on Equity	21%	35%	33%	23%	14%	12%	13%	10%	15%	29%
B09	Return on URIA	5%	5%	5%	6%	6%	6%	6%	7%	6%	5%
B09	Return on Total Capital	6%	7%	8%	7%	7%	7%	7%	7%	7%	8%
B10	Return on Equity	10%	12%	13%	15%	15%	16%	15%	15%	2%	
B10	Return on URIA	8%	7%	6%	5%	5%	5%	4%	4%	4%	
B10	Return on Total Capital	7%	8%	7%	7%	6%	7%	6%	6%	3%	
AVG	Return on Equity	14%	18%	20%	19%	17%	12%	11%	10%	10%	13%
AVG	Return on URIA	6%	6%	6%	6%	6%	7%	5%	5%	5%	3%
AVG	Return on Total Capital	7%	7%	7%	8%	8%	8%	7%	7%	7%	6%

Table 8 – Return on Capital

In a number of cases, and certainly on average, the returns on URIA appear to closely follow the interest rates that can be observed in the market. In this respect it can be argued that even though URIA display characteristics of equity, the funds obtained should be considered as operational funds, and not as a form of capital.

From section 2.3.4, it appears that the Residual Income model performs well for conventional banks. Due to the absence of market data it is, however, not possible to validate the results for Islamic banks in the same way. However, even though both capital and asset structures of Islamic banks differ from those of conventional banks, it should be possible to use the same Residual Income model as defined for conventional banks to determine the value of Islamic banks, as long as the parameters of the model are estimated correctly given the specifics of Islamic banks.

This implies that the Residual Income model provides a reliable proxy of the value of Islamic banks. In order to indicate the possible applicability of the Residual Income model to Islamic bank, the trend of value created per year of conventional banks, scaled by the book value is used as a benchmark.

The average value created by the conventional banks in the sample over the period of the research underpinning the analysis in this book is calculated using the following equation:

$$RI_t = \left(Earnings_t - (r_e \times B^e_{t-1})\right)$$

Equation 17 – Residual Income

The value thus calculated takes the perceived risk into consideration in the required return on equity (r_e), and so it is, in part, dependent on the development of the market rate of return versus the risk-free rate of return. The average value created by conventional banks over the period of this study calculated using this equation is represented in figure 2 below.

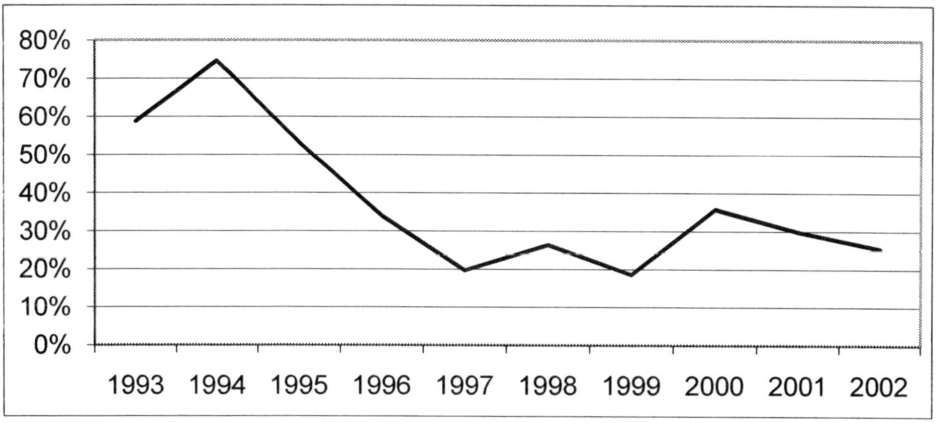

Figure 2 – Average Annual Value Creation Conventional Banks

Using the same equation, the annual value created by Islamic banks is calculated both including and excluding URIA from capital. As a result of the fact that Islamic banks and conventional banks operate in the same industry, it would be expected that the average annual value created by Islamic banks followed the same trend as that of conventional banks charted in Figure 2.

From the analysis of Islamic banks, it turns out that the inclusion of URIA as part of capital potentially provides a more realistic indication of the value of an Islamic bank than when URIA are excluded from capital. This is mainly due to the fact that, as mentioned earlier, URIA display characteristics of equity. The AAOIFI accounting regulation that has come in to effect in 2000 also treats URIA in line with equity where payout to accountholders is concerned.

Since it can be argued that inclusion of URIA provides a better indicator than the exclusion of URIA from capital, only those banks for which the amounts and payout to URIA are available are included in this part of the analysis.

In order to enable comparison with the banking industry as a whole, the resulting value created based on the Residual Income calculation for conventional banks and Islamic banks are graphed in figure 3 below.

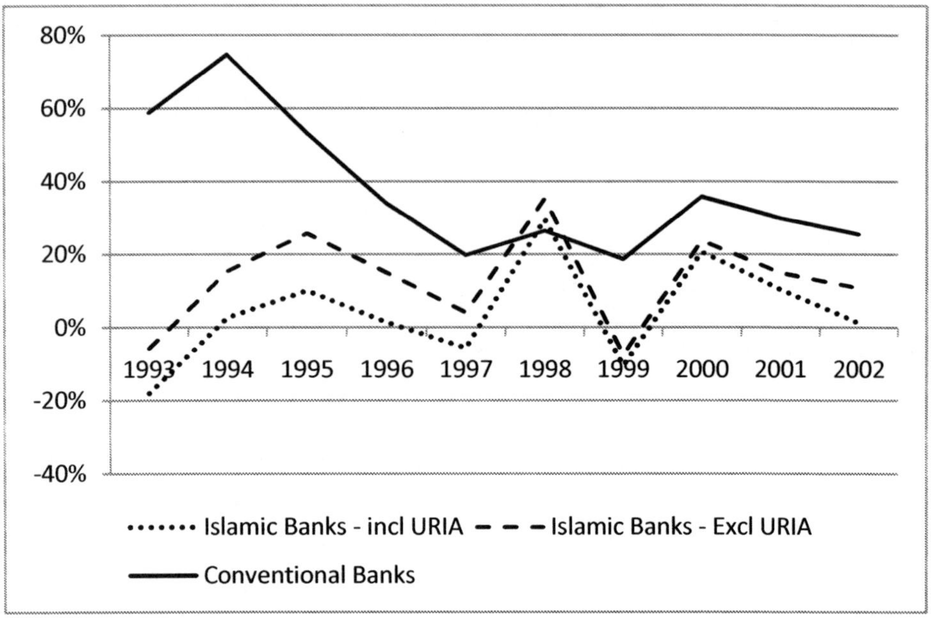

Figure 3 – Average Annual Value Creation Islamic vs Conventional Banks

As can be observed from figure 3, the Residual Income of Islamic banks, especially in later years, follows a pattern similar to that of conventional banks, but displays higher volatility. Conventional banks show an extremely high Residual Income in 1994 due to the high interest rates in that year, and the large spread between interest income and interest payment. The gap between conventional and Islamic banks becomes smaller in later years, in part due to the fact that more Islamic banks are included in the sample from 1998 onwards. The difference between including or excluding or URIA varies, but becomes smaller in later years. The differences between conventional and Islamic banks can partly be explained by the fact that the Islamic financial industry is a relative young market. However, the trend in the value creation is similar to that for conventional banks. Furthermore,

Islamic banks generally operate in what are known as weak-form efficient markets for which market data is often not available and has to be estimated using proxies.

Based on these results, the expectation is that it might be possible to use the Residual Income model as specified in equation (16) to estimate the value of an Islamic bank and then to estimate the value created using equation (16), but further research with a larger sample size and actual data rather than proxies will be required to validate this.

3.4 Valuing Islamic Banks – Myth or Reality

Although a firm conclusion cannot be drawn, due to sample size and other challenges, it appears possible to compare the value created by both types of banks as long as specific characteristics are taken into account.

It becomes clear from the analysis of Islamic bank data that the value of an Islamic bank displays more volatility when URIA are included in capital. However, this appears to be caused by the increases and decreases in the funds available for investment. Particularly during the earlier part of the research period, the returns to holders of URIA appear to closely follow the interest rates that can be observed in the market.

A number of issues have been identified which can be summarised as follows:

1. Limited sample size. The number of Islamic banks that are in existence is limited, and the sample contains only 12 banks. Furthermore, only few banks have been in operation for more than four years.
2. The implementation of AAOIFI accounting standards varies from

country-to-country. In Bahrain, the standards are mandatory, and have been since 1998. Sudan, Jordan and Qatar have recently started to make the application of AAOIFI standards mandatory. For banks in other countries the implementation of AAOIFI accounting standards is wholly voluntarily. This severely restricts the transparency of the financial statements during the period of this study, and hinders the comparability across Islamic banks.

3. URIA are in some cases treated as on-balance sheet instruments, and in others as off-balance sheet instruments, a situation that again hinders the comparability between banks. Where possible, amendments to the data have been made to include URIA on the basis of the notes the accounts. However, the information is not available in all cases.

4. Disclosure levels differ between banks, resulting in missing information that is vital for an appropriate estimation of value. For instance, profit smoothing practices, the lack of information regarding the amounts of URIA and the profits paid out to them, as well as the often summary information in the notes to the accounts are all related to the low disclosure levels.

5. Risk-free and market rates of return as well as company β data are generally not available and proxies need to be determined.

6. Analyst consensus growth estimations are not available, and estimates for the one-year, two-year, and long-term growth forecast have to be made based on historical growth data.

The low reliability and comparability of the financial statement data, in combination with the extensive use of proxy information, and the limited sample size result in the situation that the suitability of the Residual Income model to determine the value of Islamic banks cannot be demonstrated in the same way as for conventional banks, and it is therefore almost impossible to draw definitive conclusions.

Furthermore, the market is relatively immature, which further reduces the potential ability to apply a Residual Income model. However, the findings suggest that the Residual Income model can be applied to compare the value of Islamic banks. There is also the potential to apply the model so that comparisons can be made with conventional banks, once the issues identified in this chapter have been resolved.

4 Further Observations

Numerous studies have identified the Residual Income model, outlined in the previous chapters, to work as a viable valuation approach for non-banks using stock-market valuations as a benchmark. Each of these studies has specifically excluded financial institutions. However, as the results in the previous chapters show, it is indeed possible to apply the Residual Income model to both conventional and Islamic banks to provide a reasonable valuation.

When the value of a conventional bank is estimated using the Residual Income model as defined in equation (16), the results show a high correlation between the market price and the estimated value, and thus the value explains a large percentage of cross-sectional variations in market prices. The goodness of fit of the results is around 80% at a confidence level of 99%. As a result, similar to companies in non-financial industries, it can be argued that the model provides a robust indication of the value of a conventional bank, given its perceived risk as compared to the market portfolio.

Historically, Islamic and conventional finance have developed based on the same core principle, which is to provide financial intermediation between holders of surplus funds and those requiring funds for investment. Apart from the fact that Islamic finance operates based on the principles of the *Qur'an,* which prohibits both interest and speculation, the main difference between the Islamic and conventional banking industry is related to the further development of the industries. Where the first conventional banks started in the 17th century, Islamic banks only started operating in their current form in 1963. Because the Islamic banking industry as we know it now is still relatively young, there are a number of issues related to availability and transparency of data. Moreover, Islamic banks predominantly operate in countries where the capital market is not fully developed, so that share prices for such banks are either not set in an efficient market setting or not available at all.

The results of the study outlined in the previous chapter indicate that it is, in principle, possible to apply the Residual Income model to Islamic banks, although a number of issues will need to be resolved, which can be summarised as follows:

- Non-availability of market data;
- Restricted sample size;
- Requirement to use proxies;
- Lack of transparency of accounting information.

Each of these issues will need to be resolved before more definite conclusions can be drawn regarding the application of the model in practice. Support for the validation of the results can be found in the comparison of the average value created by Islamic banks and conventional banks, which shows a similar trend although the results for Islamic banks are more volatile than the ones for conventional banks, especially in earlier years.

Besides Islamic financial institutions there are other relatively small sections in the financial industry such as micro finance and socially responsible investing, both even smaller than the estimated $1 trillion of the Islamic finance industry. Whether the model can be extended to include these parts of the financial industry falls outside the scope of this book, but a few observations can be made. Both micro finance and socially responsible finance attract a significant amount of interest and, like Islamic finance, find their basis in a set of ethical principles.

1. Micro Finance

Micro credit is the provision of loans to the unemployed, poor entrepreneurs and others living in poverty that are generally deemed to be un-bankable. They typically lack collateral, steady employment and credit history and, therefore, do not have access to traditional means of credit. Traditional banks see these borrowers as high risk and don't want to extend credit. Interestingly enough, micro credit is often extended to women to engage in self-employment projects that allow them to generate income. The loans are very small. To put it all in perspective, when Muhammad Yunus started Grameen Bank, he extended a total of $27 in loans which he lent to 42 people. In order to enhance the chance of repayment, micro credit institutions often use a system of "solidarity groups". They provide a support network for each other's efforts, as well as some social pressure. In combination with active management and extensive support for clients, around 90% of the loans are repaid on time and in full. Although a cost intensive operation, it is also one of reduced credit risk. Further costs are incurred when it comes to regulatory capital requirements. Due to the fact that the transactions are typically not backed by collateral, the risk profile is deemed to be higher resulting in additional capital requirements. Additional cost occur due to the potentially high transaction volume, particularly low transaction size and operational costs per transaction that are at least the same compared with larger financial transactions. On the other hand, micro credit clients don't only take credit, they also save therefore creating a co-operative or building society type institution.

2. **Socially Responsible Investing**

Socially Responsible or ethical investing is concerned with investing in sustainable and environmentally-friendly opportunities. It seeks to maximise financial return as well as the social good. Socially responsible investors generally favour corporations that promote environmental stewardship, consumer protection, human rights and diversity. Some investors avoid businesses involved in alcohol, gambling, weapons and other industries. The decision to include or exclude any investment lies with the individual investor. In itself, socially responsible investing is not a new phenomenon. In 1690, John Fraeme and Thomas Gould started trading as Goldsmith

> Bankers in Lombard Street (London, United Kingdom) and subsequently incorporated the name Barclay in 1736 when the son in law of one of the founders became a partner in the business. Over time, this developed into Barclays Bank. In 1765, John Taylor and Sampson Lloyd started Lloyds bank in Birmingham (United Kingdom). Both Barclays and Lloyds are examples of banks whose business was strongly rooted in the puritan values that came with their Quaker heritage and which are largely similar to the principles underlying socially responsible investing.

Neither socially responsible investing nor micro finance are non-profit. On the contrary, both are concerned with making a profit within the framework of their operations and associated principles. As such, it should be equally possible to apply a residual income model to determine the value of these financial institutions, as long as their specific business model is taken into consideration.

Part 2 – In Uncertain Times

Challenges in Uncertain Times

> *"Pursue a straightforward, upright, legitimate banking business. Never be tempted by the prospect of large returns to do anything but what may properly be done under the National Currency Act. Splendid financiering is not legitimate banking and splendid financiers are generally either humbugs or rascals." Hugh McCulloch, 1st Comptroller of the Currency, 1863*[23]

At the time of writing of this book in early 2009 it was no longer a certainty that big banks would be around forever and as many journalists and politicians kept on insisting the financial industry as we knew it had come to an end. Subprime mortgages and excessive risk taking has resulted in the bankruptcy of Lehman Brothers and the mass nationalisation of banks around the world. Everything we know about the financial industry including the regulatory environment has been questioned. Was it all the fault of the bankers? Probably not. Was all of it the regulator's fault then? Probably not either. Is it, as some would like us to believe, unique in the history of finance? Not even that.

Interestingly enough, as the "Grumpy Old Bankers"[24] point out, there is nothing new about this crisis; we have seen it all before. From the Tulip bubble in the 1600's via the South Sea bubble, the dot.com boom and the subprime crisis, asset inflation has been part of the financial industry just as much as Asset Backed Securities, Premium Bonds and Government Debt.

Part 2 of this book, highlights a few of the issues associated with valuation of banks in these uncertain times. Did the Value at Risk measure work and if not, why not? What is the impact of news on stock

---

[23] Centre for the Study of Financial Innovation (CSFI), 2009 *Grumpy Old Bankers: Wisdom from Crisis Past*. London: CSFI, page 10

[24] As above

prices, and how does behavioural finance come into play? These questions, as well as the possible use of the Residual Income model to predict asset bubbles, will be reviewed in this section.

5 The Challenge with Value at Risk

"The story that I have to tell is marked all the way through by a persistent tension between those who assert that the best decisions are based on quantification and numbers, determined by the patterns of the past, and those who base their decisions on more subjective degrees of belief about the uncertain future. This is a controversy that has never been resolved." Peter L. Bernstein – *Against the Gods*[25]

Although initially devised as a measure to report financial risks, Value at Risk, or VaR as it is most commonly known, was soon used to attempt to measure the downside risk of either a portfolio or, in aggregation, a firm into one single number. It is very much a numbers-based methodology based on past patterns. The output of a VaR equation attempts to measure the downside risk taking into account financial leverage and diversification effects across all markets and instruments. It represents the maximum amount a bank is likely to stand to lose on a given day or over a number of days (e.g. over a period of one week), generally with a confidence interval of 95% or 99%.

There are three main types of VaR, each with their own strengths and weaknesses:

- **Historical VaR**. The Historical VaR estimates the nth percentile in potential losses based on historical returns on the relevant traded assets. Historical VaR measures potential portfolio risk one to two years ahead using the previous few years (typically anywhere between one and twenty, but more often than not spanning one to two years) as a benchmark.

---

[25] Bernstein, Peter L. (1998) *Against the Gods: The Remarkable Story of Risk* New York: John Wiley & Sons

- **Variance-Covariance VaR**. The Variance-Covariance VaR takes the historical volatility and correlation of returns on traded assets into consideration when calculating the nth percentile in potential losses. Variance-Covariance VaR is again typically based on historic data covering a period of two to ten years.
- **Monte Carlo VaR**. Monte Carlo is a commonly used simulation technique which is used to simulate a variety of different scenarios for the portfolio value on the target date. The Monte Carlo VaR method approximates the behaviour of financial prices using simulations to generate random price paths. The result is a forward-looking simulation of the environment, rather than using historical data like Historical and Variance-Covariance VaR.

Over time, banks started to use VaR as a risk control tool. Trading limits were complemented by VaR limits, and at a firm level it was used to control firm-wide risk-taking diversification into account. From an initially passive tool, it started to develop into a tool to control risk and subsequently into a risk allocation tool. It is designed to incorporate traditional risks and risks related to adverse market movements of financial derivatives and structured products. In addition, VaR is often used as a basis to calculate the amount of economic capital required to support a business, which is an essential component of economic value added measures.

5.1 The Beauty of VaR

No matter which VaR framework is used, the result of the equation provides a single amount that is deemed to be the maximum value a bank is exposed to over the coming period – generally one week or ten days – with a very high level of confidence. For example, a one-week VaR of $100 million with a 99% confidence level indicates that there is a 99% chance that the portfolio will not lose more than $100 million over the next week.

Another advantage of VaR is that is can measure risks at different levels very quickly. It can be applied to individual contracts, portfolios, a trader's position but also firm-wide, and can generally be made available within a short time.

Because of these advantages, banks used the VaR to meet the Securities and Exchange Committee (SEC) requirements for quantitative disclosure of market risk in the financial statement. The Basel Committee on Banking Supervision went even further and allowed banks to rely on their own internal VaR calculations to define capital requirements to support market risk.

5.2 How VaR has Fared

Although implemented widely, VaR has not necessarily fared very well during the current crisis for a number of reasons. Generally, most implementations of VaR assume that the portfolio of assets and liabilities that are part of the analysis stays constant over the one-period or 10-day horizon. On January the 28th 2008, Bloomberg.com[26] reported that at a time that Merrill Lynch's reported losses on CDOs had already reached $18 billion, their historical VaR was reported to be $92 million. How does this occur, and what is the issue with VaR?

First of all, VaR mainly provides an indication of the maximum risk a bank is exposed to under the assumption that the distribution of the underlying price data is approximately normal, which, as we know, is not necessarily the case. In addition, the question of what happens outside the confidence interval (e.g. the other 1%) is not really addressed. But that is exactly where the current issues come from, at least in part. These incidents are commonly referred to as "Black

26 Death of VAR Evoked as Risk Taking Vim Meets Taleb's Black Swan

Swans"[27]. A Black Swan is defined as an incident that is incredibly rare and is therefore not considered a possibility. Take for example the collapse of Long Term Capital Management (LTCM) which was due to the fact that under normal market circumstances the Asian and the Russian crisis could not have occurred simultaneously. When the market did not return to what was considered to be "normal" but LTCM was still trading as if it would, they eventually went bust.

There are other challenges associated with the VaR methodology. VaR relies heavily on historical data which does not necessarily repeat itself. In addition, the historical data generally only covers a relatively short period, which in turn implies that extreme circumstances are not necessary taken into consideration.

Box 8 – The Use of Historic Data, An Example

A significant amount of the implementations of VaR apply a two-year historic data period to determine the Value at Risk. The VaR on a sub prime mortgage portfolio would have been much higher than the actual risk incurred due to the fact that during the period 2006 – 2007 house prices did not decrease. If a longer period of historic data had been used which would have included the previous house price crash of 1989, the value at risk on the same portfolio is likely to have been significantly larger. Although, even then, the accuracy of the resulting VaR number may not have been correct.

---

[27] The theory was described by Nassim Nicholas Taleb in his 2007 book *The Black Swan*. The term *Black Swan* comes from the assumption that 'All swans are white'. In that context, a *black swan* was a symbol for something that could not exist. The 18th Century discovery of black swans in Western Australia was first used by John Stuart Mill to illustrate that a perceived impossibility can be contradicted by a new discovery.

The impact of adverse movements in available liquidity is not included in the assumptions underlying the model, which is another reason why VaR underperforms in the current crisis. The significant reduction in liquidity and the associated widening of credit spreads is not something that is typically included in the analysis as a likely scenario. The London Interbank Offer Rate (LIBOR) has always been assumed to have a small spread over government paper and futures, an assumption that was disproved during the late 2008 and 2009 credit crunch when the LIBOR rates quoted were well in excess of the central banks' base rates. On top of that, the rates actually charged by banks in the capital markets were significantly higher than the LIBOR rates quoted. Institutions heavily relying on the capital markets for their funding such as Northern Rock and HBOS in the United Kingdom were either forced into nationalisation or being taken over. Their business models, which relied on arbitrage between the interest on retail mortgages and the cost of funds in the capital markets, failed as a result of the inverted yield curves.

Banks are particularly susceptible to systematic risk, which is the risk posed to the financial system or the (global) economy. The failure of a major financial institution can result in a domino effect throughout the financial industry which has the potential to bring down an economy. Not only will their depositors lose any money that is not covered by a guarantee scheme, they are also likely to renege on their obligations as counterparties towards other financial institutions. This, in turn, will result in financial pressures on these individuals and institutions that may subsequently have to renege on some of their obligations and so on and so forth. Given a global financial infrastructure, this can potentially have far reaching consequences.

Box 9 – The Far Reaching Impact of Non-Settlement

In June 1974, a small, relatively unknown bank in Germany, Bank Herstatt, had its banking licence withdrawn and was ordered into liquidation effective the close of the German interbank payments system at 3:30 in the afternoon on the 26th of June 1974. During the morning before Herstatt's banking licence was withdrawn, some of their counterparties had made irrevocable payments in Deutsche Mark to satisfy their payment obligations in foreign exchange transactions against US Dollars. These payments were made in good faith in the anticipation of the receipt of the US Dollar equivalent later that day. When Herstatt's licence was withdrawn at 3:30 in the afternoon German time, it was only 10:30 in the morning in New York. The correspondent bank suspended all outgoing US Dollar payments with immediate effect, leaving Herstatt's counterparties fully exposed to the value of the Deutsche Mark paid earlier that day, without any receipt of the corresponding amounts in US Dollar. Subsequently, some of the counterparties could not directly fulfil the US Dollar obligations they had to other parties resulting in a domino effect.

VaR does not really incorporate the effects of a global, highly correlated financial market. On the contrary, VaR typically assumes that assets are liquid and can easily be sold at, or at least near, the current market value. In the event that a financial institution has to liquidate assets urgently to realise capital, the law of demand and supply dictates that the price will be negatively impacted, which is a result of higher supply at a consistent or lower level of demand. This has a further negative effect on the bank being able to meet its obligations.

Looking at the current crisis, another challenge associated with VaR is that many of the losses in the current crisis have occurred on assets that are non-traded such as subprime mortgage loans, Alt-A mortgages[28] and structured products that use the former as reference collateral. Because they are non-traded, they are often not included in the VaR calculations, with all the associated consequences. Subprime and Alt-A mortgages packaged up in Mortgage Backed Securities (MBS) were generally assigned a high credit rating, in part justified by the diversification effect. However, under the US mortgage regime, a lender can easily put the house back to the bank when the value of the house declines. Subprime mortgages, typically, have low deposits and the chance of default is generally higher than with other mortgages.

The VaR calculation also assumes that the portfolio will remain unchanged. No assets will mature, and no assets will either be bought or sold. Although this may be a workable assumption for a very short time period, in a market where trades take place on a near continuous basis, it is highly unlikely. And if all that was not enough, the Monte Carlo VaR assumes that the returns in a period are independent from the previous period, which is a flawed concept. The majority of returns are highly cyclical and will be dependent on previous period returns, particularly when considering potential defaults or price movements. Finally, VaR involves estimations of future values, correlation and other factors each of which can result in estimation errors.

Overall, it would be safe to say that VaR has many disadvantages. These appear to be mainly associated with events that, to say the least, can be considered to be unusual. But still, the high confidence level appears to have resulted in a false sense of security

---

[28] Alt-A stands for Alternative A paper. Alt-A mortgages are a type of US mortgage which are riskier than prime mortgages due to conditions such as a lower credit score, a higher loan-to-value or because they are extended on investment properties

5.3 Is VaR all bad?

Boldly saying that VaR is all bad and should never be used again is probably a classic case of throwing the baby out with the bathwater. There is a lot to say against VaR. The use of short term historic data, the black swans, the fact that non traded instruments are not included are all issues that may need to be addressed. However, it does provide a single number that is easy to understand. Although it may be flawed, it is still the best number out there when it comes to a firm's risk. The next question will then have to be "where to from here?"

First, the VaR methodology could be enhanced significantly if issues such as recognition of cyclicality and defaults and the inclusion of non-traded assets is to be addressed. On the other hand, this may potentially be an expensive exercise and could lead to other challenges. In addition, the VaR number should probably be given a lot less individual importance. Rather than looking at the output on a day-to-day basis, the trend is where changes in risk will be spotted that can then be analysed further. VaR is not an all-knowing methodology; it would have to be used as a tool in combination with other risk management tools such as, for instance, Risk Adjusted Return on Capital (RAROC), the purpose of which is to adjust trading profits by the remuneration of risk capital. RAROC recognises that trading positions with a higher risk profile require a larger amount of economic capital to absorb larger potential losses. If we remember that VaR does not look at what could happen in the other 1% of the time, and keep the liquidity of the instruments as well as the markets in mind it can still play a significant role in the overall risk assessment process.

In any case, any risk taken by a bank will have to be evaluated against its risk management system, as well as the cost of the measures in place. The complexity of banks seriously hinders simple assessment of the risks taken and how they are controlled. It will never be possible to incorporate safeguards against all risks within the risk management system of a bank. A more complex risk management system may actually make the situation worse, due to the increasing complexity that is introduced, as well as potentially creating a false sense of security.

IN UNCERTAIN TIMES

6 The Impact of News and Behavioural Finance

Valuation models generally assume that investors exhibit rational behaviour when they make their investment decisions. The severe reductions in stock prices that occurred during the second half of 2008 and early 2009, however, support the theory that investors may react to news in a way that is not purely based on fundamental values. This chapter explores the Efficient Market Hypothesis, behavioural finance and the response of investors to news.

6.1 Efficient Market Hypothesis

The efficient market hypothesis is based on the notion that all available information is directly incorporated in the price of a security, and arbitrage based on information is therefore impossible. Nearly all valuation and asset pricing theories assume that the market behaves in this way. Over time, research has shown that not all markets are equally efficient, and three forms of the efficient market hypothesis can be distinguished[29]:

Weak-form efficient market

In a weak-form efficient market, it is not possible for an investor to earn excess returns by developing trading rules based on historical price or return information. In these markets, any information available beyond historical prices and returns is not necessarily reflected in the share price. Whether this information is publicly available or not is irrelevant, and trading typically takes place on the basis of information available to the individual investor which could include insider information. In these markets, investors can enhance their returns by implementing a trading

[29] Copeland, T.E and J.F. Weston (1992) *Financial Theory and Corporate Policy* Third Edition, New York: Addison Wesley Publishing Company

strategy of seeking out over- or undervalued stocks.

Semi-strong form efficient market

In a semi-strong-form efficient market, all publicly available information is immediately and fully reflected in the share price. Trading strategies seeking out over- or undervalued stocks will only result in a potential profit for the investor if he has insider information available to him.

Strong-form efficient market

In a strong-form efficient market, all publicly available information is immediately and fully reflected in the share price and insider trading is prohibited. The prohibition of insider trading is generally implemented within a legal and/or regulatory framework. Investors can not earn any excess returns purely based on company information available to them.

Results of event studies have indicated that stock prices generally tend to adjust quickly to information about investment decisions, dividend changes, changes in capital structure, and corporate control transactions. All of these findings support the semi-strong-form of the efficient market hypothesis concluding that any publicly available information will be incorporated in the share price almost instantaneously. However, the majority of these studies have been executed in American and European markets, where value-relevant private information appears to be rare, and where markets are classified as semi-strong-form efficient.

In emerging markets, however, prices do not necessarily reflect all available information. Trading is often restricted to a few hours per day. Kuwait Stock Exchange's trading hours, for example, are 9:15 – 12:15 for the Spot Market and 12:45 – 13:15 for the Futures Market, and Bahrain Stock Exchange's trading hours are 10:00 – 13:00. Not all stocks are traded on a daily basis and both volume and value of trades are typically quite low. In addition, purchase and sale decisions are often driven by personal motives such as how well someone gets on with the chairman of a company and not necessarily on private or public information. The characteristics of these markets result in the fact that they cannot be classified as efficient, potentially not even in its weakest form. Fama[30] has done extensive research into the effectiveness of markets and found as early as 1970 that "The current price of a security 'fully reflects' all available information", and thus that there is such a thing as an efficient market. This forms the basis for the Random Walk Theory of weak-form efficiency.[31] Only when extensive testing appeared to support the efficiency hypothesis at this level, did research move on to semi-strong and strong-form tests.

6.2 Behavioural Finance

The conventional banks that are part of the underlying study are all based in semi strong-form efficient markets where prices are deemed to incorporate all available information quickly. However, the severe price changes in the current market circumstances further confirm the findings in behavioural finance that the agents in the market are not necessarily rational. After all, as early as 1912, Selden[32] wrote *Psychology of the Stock Market* "upon the belief that the movements of prices on the exchanges are dependent to a very considerable degree on the mental attitude of the investing and trading public".

In 1957, Simon[33] introduced the concept of bounded rationality which

---

[30] Fama, E.F. (1970) *Efficient Capital Markets: A Review of Theory and Empirical Work,* The Journal of Finance, 25(2), 383-417

[31] The Random Walk Theory states that the entire distribution is independent of the information available. Initial studies on efficient markets were further concerned with weak-form efficient markets in which the information subset of interest is just past price (or return) histories.

[32] Selden, G. C., (1912) *Psychology of the Stock Market: Human Impulses Lead To Speculative Disasters*. New York: Ticker Publishing.

[33] Simon, Herbert (1957). *Models of Man, Social and Rational: Mathematical Essays*

recognises that people do not base all their decisions on fact but are influenced by other elements. The human mind has limitations and does not have the capacity to understand everything, particularly when complexity increases. In addition, there is only limited time available in which to reach decisions and people are generally influenced by the perceived quality of a news source. As a result, Simon argues that decisions are not fully thought through and people can only be rational within limits.

Research by Boston College, Massachusets[34], shows that public news releases can have a significant impact on the price of different types of U.S. Treasury bonds. Out of a number of news issues available such as Nonfarm payroll, and the change in unemployment level, consumer price index and the Treasury budget, only those are selected that are deemed to be surprising, i.e. where the news is either better or worse than generally expected by the market. Although the effects of these surprise announcements vary according to maturity, public news can explain a substantial portion of price volatility during the period almost immediately following the announcement. This particular research finds that prices move significantly before any increase in volume is observed, which creates the suggestion that the initial price adjustment is mainly driven by public information. Trading volume and price volatility increases have been observed to persist for around 60 minutes, but the bid-ask spreads reverted back to normal after about 15 minutes after the announcement. This in itself suggests that a second phase of price adjustments exists during which both volatility and volume are partly driven by informed trading. Even beyond the 15

---

on Rational Human Behavior in a Social Setting. New York: Wiley.

[34] Balduzzi, P., J.E. Elton and T.C. Green (2001) *Economic News and Bond Prices: Evidence from the U.S. treasury Market*, Journal of Financial and Quantitative Analysis, Vol 36, No 4, pp 523 – 543 Seattle: University of Washington School of Business Administration

minute period trading persists at an above average level. These findings support earlier research, which find similar reactions to news for other asset classes such as futures[35].

A more recent study by Roache and Rossi[36] shows that unexpected announcement of economic indicators have an almost direct impact on the prices of various commodities, although the exact impact varies according to the type of commodity. One of their main findings is that gold prices react to specific scheduled announcements in the United States and the Euro area (e.g. indicators of activity such as the employment data and payroll or interest rate decisions). They find that the way in which the Gold price reacts is consistent with its traditional role as a safe-haven and store of value. In contrast, which is contrary to the response of other commodity prices to significant news items.

Previous literature on the impact of macroeconomic announcements has mostly focussed on bond and currency markets, but there is fairly clear and consistent evidence that macroeconomic news has significant price and volatility effects. In some cases the reaction happens on the same day, but in other cases the impact is not visible until the next day. Although a large range of macroeconomic data is made publicly available, the impact on prices appears particularly significant in periods when uncertainty is high and when the news is related to the labour market, inflation and durable goods orders. Although the majority of academic research in this area is reviewing the impact of macroeconomic announcements on bond and currency markets, it is by no means a long stretch to imagine the impact news generally may have on other commodities and equity prices.

---

[35] Ederington, L. H., and J. H. Lee (1993) *How Markets Process Information: News Releases and Volatility* Journal of Finance, Vol 48, pp 1161-1191.

[36] Roache, Shaun K. and M. Rossi (2009) *The Effects of Economic News on Commodity Prices: Is Gold Just Another Commodity?* IMF Working paper 09/140, Washington: IMF

It is not just macroeconomic news the market responds to. In 1996 Allan Greenspan, then chairman of the Federal Reserve Board coined the term *irrational exuberance* to describe the behavior of stock market investors[37] in a televised speech in Washington. As soon as these words were mentioned stock markets dropped (Nikkei Index -3.2%, Hang Seng -2.9%, DAX -4%, FTSE -4% and the Dow Jones -2.3%) without any apparent reason. Robert Schiller[38] has since researched this issue further and concludes that the term itself has become useful to characterise the social phenomenon that occurs when markets have been bid up to unusually high and unsustainable levels under the influence of a naïve and optimistic market psychology. The sharp drop in share prices globally in late 2008/early 2009 was, at least in part, a case of correcting for earlier *"irrational exuberance"*. Considerable numbers of stocks were overvalued and a market correction was at that point long overdue. The significant price drop cannot, however, be explained entirely by a market correction. The initial news surrounding Lehman's bankruptcy caused investors to sell banking shares at heavily discounted prices. It soon became apparent that financial institutions that had previously announced positive profit expectations might actually have sustained significant losses. Due to a lack of transparency, increasing complexity of the financial instruments underpinning the crisis and the fact that no one appeared to know who was exposed to the credit risk on securitised financial assets, the extent of the losses that were sustained did not become clear until much later, adding even more uncertainty. Banks were nationalised or forced to take over other entities again which caused yet another layer of uncertainty. Investors responded to all the uncertainty perhaps excessively or even

---

[37] Greenspan, A. (1996) *The Challenge of Central Banking in a Democratic Society,* speech before the American Enterprise Institute for Public Policy, Washington, 5th December 1996

[38] Schiller, R.J. (2005) *Irrational Exuberance* second edition, Princeton, New Jersey: Princeton University Press

irrationally, but this is not necessarily unexpected and is in part associated with herd behaviour and reliance on certain news sources. Herd behaviour is however not necessarily irrational, especially when the investor is trading on someone else's behalf. Consider for instance a situation in which a trader decides to buy bank shares at a time when everyone else is selling. If he gets it right, he's a hero, but getting it wrong can have severe consequences. Contrary, would buying bank shares being an acceptable strategy followed by many and it goes wrong the individual typically does not get "punished" for his decision.

Box 10 - How media may influence investors

An interesting example of the influence of media on share prices is the Mad Money programme on CNBC. Various pieces of research have found[39] that the stock recommendations provided on the programme generally do not appear to outperform the market. Although no one can beat the market consistently, the buy and sell recommendations given on the Mad Money programme appear to lead to a consistent underperformance. Statistics show, however, that investors seem to act on the recommendations provided in the programme. It is unclear whether this is because they trust Cramer's decisions or whether investors take some form of comfort from the fact that the programme is broadcast by CNBC. In any case, it does show that not all investment decisions are rational. If investors would act rationally, they would undertake their own fundamental analysis as well and make an informed decision on whether to invest or not and not just act on the word of one man.

[39] Alpert, B (2009) *Cramer's Star Outshines his Stock Picks* and *The Cramer Effect – and Defect* (February 2007), both of which also mention additional research. The articles were published on www.smartmoney.com/investing.

6.3 Is the Market Efficient?

Ultimately, investors do not base their investment decisions solely on fundamental analysis and available information. They rely on heuristics[40], the perceived credibility of the news source and other emotional and factors associated with perception[41]. Among the findings of a variety of research are the following:

- Long-term earnings forecasts made by security analysts tend to be biased toward recent successes;
- Analysts tend to be more optimistic about recent winners than recent losers;
- Investors have different attitudes to risk, which influences the individual's decision process.
- When making decisions under uncertainty, people tend to apply what is known as the *Minimax Regret Criterion.* Given a choice most people are biased towards avoiding a certain loss, but will take a chance on a smaller loss since the probability of loss reduction has a strong attraction to the decision maker. Under uncertainty, the decision maker measures the opportunity cost (regret) associated with each possible course of action and selects the action that minimises the maximum regret. Regret is in this case measured as the difference between the best and the worst outcome for each course of action.

There are more examples of how emotions and perceptions influence investor decisions and hence share prices. Behavioural finance certainly

---

[40] The process by which people find out things for themselves, usually by trial and error.

[41] For further reading see for example Shefrin, H (2002) *Beyond Greed and Fear: Understanding Behavioral Finance and the Psychology of Investing.* Oxford: Oxford University Press.

plays a role when it comes to share prices.

However, despite all of the evidence to the contrary discussed above, the efficient market theory still plays a significantly larger part in the valuation of firms. Generally, research into the area has established that 80% of a company's share price is determined based on the fundamental value estimated of the firm which is estimated using, for instance, a Residual Income Model. This leaves only 20% or less open to investment decisions on elements other than fundamental value. In addition, the impact of behavioural finance is typically only noticed during a brief period. Share prices generally appear to be reverting back to the value based on their fundamental value after a relatively short period of time. All in all, although behavioural finance has some influence on share price movements, but the bulk of the price is still made up of the estimated (future) value of a firm, particularly over the longer term.

7 Can Asset Bubbles be Predicted?

"I cannot calculate the madness of the people" Sir Isaac Newton on the South Sea Bubble[42]

The asset bubble is just not a modern phenomenon, but has been around for a long time, with the first recorded bubble, Tulip Mania, raging in Holland from 1624 to 1636. At its start the man from Amsterdam who owned the only specimens in Holland was offered 3,000 florins for a single bulb, which, at the time, was around the average annual income of a wealthy merchant. At its height, three rare tulip bulbs changed hands for a farmhouse. To put it all into perspective, in 1642 Rembrandt van Rijn was commissioned to paint *"De compagnie van kapitein Frans Banninck Cocq en luitenant Willem van Ruytenburch maakt zich gereed om uit te marcheren"*[43], which is better known as *The Night Watch*, and originally measured about 3.8 by 4.54m. It is believed that he was paid around 1,600 florins for this painting, or just over half of what was paid for the tulip bulb mentioned earlier.

More bubbles followed after Tulip Mania, most notably the South Sea Bubble which caused Sir Isaac Newton to state in despair that he could not calculate the madness of the people. Interestingly enough, he was not referring to just any investors. Sir Isaac Newton allegedly lost £20,000 (equating to roughly £3 million in today's money) in the South Sea Bubble himself. Of all people he really should have known better – he did, after all, invent the mathematics that could expose the impossibility of the South Sea Company's promise of returns to be paid

[42] As quoted by Thomas Levenson "Commentary: Even a genius can get suckered", CNN Policits.com 29 July 2009

[43] The Company of captain Frans Banninck Cocq and lieutenant Willem van Ruytenburch are getting ready to march.

to an everlasting stream of new investors. Many bubbles followed, but none as well documented as the Great Depression, which was triggered by the 1929 US Stock Market Crash and was only named *"Depression"* because the alternative term would be *"Panic"* which was deemed inappropriate[44]. Unfortunately, there are no signs that we have collectively learned our lesson from any of these or, for that matter, subsequent asset bubbles such as the Dot.Com boom (and subsequent bust) and the Credit Crunch clearly show. Similar to Tulip Mania, the South Sea Bubble and the Great Depression, each of these was intensified by a combination of greed and a strong belief that this time it was all going to be different.

Reviewing the history of asset bubbles it becomes clear they do not seem to appear overnight. It takes a few years for the momentum to build up. The inevitable bust on the other hand is much more immediate and can occur in a very short period. Take, for example, the start of the Great Depression. A few days before the stock market crash, Professor Irving Fisher, not the least respected economist of his time, stated that *"Stock prices have reached what looks like a permanently high plateau"*, which was followed by his observation on the 21st of October that the market was *"only shaking out of the lunatic fringe"* and explained he felt that prices had still not caught up with their real value and should go much higher. As late as one day before the famous crash of the 24th of October 1929, he even stated that *"security values in most instances were not inflated"*.

More recently, in June 2007, Gordon Brown congratulated the City of London on its remarkable achievements and *"an era that history will record as the beginning of a new golden age"*[45] in his last speech as

---

44 Brendon, P (2009) *With Bubbles, it's plus ça change...* Financial World, July/August 2009, London: CSFI

45 Speech by the Chancellor of the Exchequer, the Rt Hon Gordon Brown MP, to Mansion House. http://www.hm-treasury.gov.uk/press_68_07.htm

Chancellor of the Exchequer of the United Kingdom.

Does this mean we collectively did not see it coming, or did we just decide to close our eyes to the inevitable? After all, business was good and profits were high. Maybe, just maybe, everything really would be different this time around and stock prices had actually reached a new, sustainable plateau. Unfortunately, it turned out that what seemed too good to be true was indeed too good to be true and in the end this also was a bubble that had to burst. In March 2008 JP Morgan took over Bear Sterns after intervention by the US Federal Reserve (FED). Allowing Bear Sterns to fail was deemed to be unsuitable due to the domino effect it would have on the financial system. By September of the same year, Lehman Brothers collapsed when the FED decided not to intervene but allow the bank to go bankrupt and let other banks pick up (some of) the pieces. Shock waves went through the financial system, but the collapse of Lehman had one major advantage. The full extent of the crisis became clear a lot faster than it would have done if Lehman's would have been rescued. Rescuing Lehman Brothers would have only delayed the inevitable.

7.1 What Recent Data Tells Us

Hindsight is a wonderful thing, and many have seriously believed that there was indeed a new economic order. The question that arises is whether it would have been possible to predict, or at least foresee, events leading up to the credit crunch or the Great Depression by applying fundamental analysis. From the results presented in Chapter 2, it has become apparent that share price inflation in the run-up to a crisis reduces the goodness of fit of the Residual Income Model which measures how closely the estimated fundamental value matches the share price. In the run-up to an asset bubble, the spread between the share price and the estimated fundamental value widens, and as a result the goodness of fit reduces. During the period of the original study from 1993 until 2002, two crises occurred reasonably close after each other, the Asian crisis, closely followed by the Dot.com boom. During the period 2003 – 2007 the global financial sector built itself up towards the biggest crisis since the Great Depression. In this section, a longer period of data is used to evaluate how price and estimated value have fared over time.

7.1.1 The Data

Between 2003 and 2008, a total number of eighty banks that were part of the original sample have either voluntarily or mandatorily merged with other institutions or have ceased to exist altogether. As a result, no data is available from Datastream on these entities. Mellon Financial for instance merged with Bank of New York in 2008 and although the key financial data can be obtained from their annual report filing (report 10K) with the Securities and Exchange Commission (SEC), the analyst consensus forecast data is no longer available. Similar to the construction of the original sample outlined in section 2.3, these entities have been removed from the total sample, resulting in a total sample of 114 banks for which sufficient data is available up to and including the end of December 2008. Added to this sample is ABN AMRO Bank for which, due to a takeover, data is available up to the end of December 2007, but no data is recorded for the year 2008. However, the impact of ABN AMRO's operations in 2008 is proportionally represented in the results of the banks that were part of the consortium that bought the bank. The total sample size used here is therefore 115.

7.1.2 The Statistics

Using panel data analysis, the test results for the original period spanning 1993 – 2002 showed that the fundamental value estimated using the Residual Income Model explains in excess of 80% of the price with a 99% probability. Extending this period to end in 2008, unsurprisingly results in a slightly lower explanatory value but, even given the tumultuous circumstances starting early 2007, over the period it can still be concluded that in excess of 78% of the share price is based on the estimated fundamental value.

Looking at the average price and estimated fundamental value for all 115 banks in the sample, over the period, it becomes clear how the observed deterioration in the goodness of fit between price and estimated fundamental value occurs.

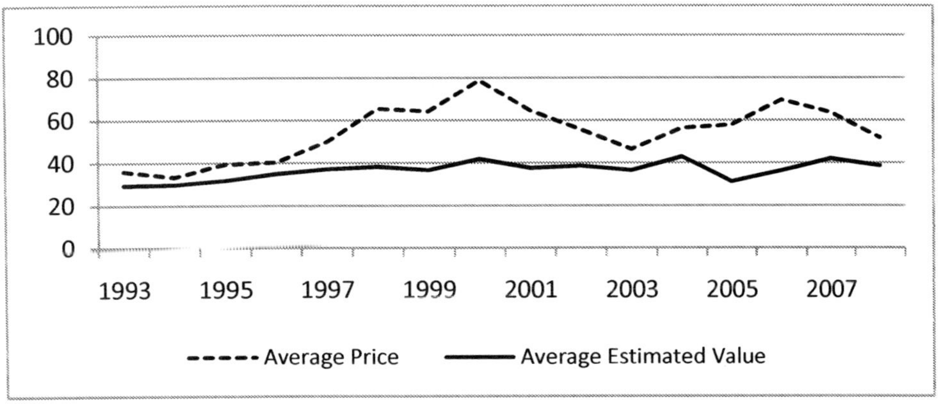

Figure 4 – Average price and average estimated fundamental value 1993 – 2008 (in $mn)

Figure 4 above, clearly shows a steep increase in prices from around 1996 to 1998, with the average estimated fundamental value remaining roughly at the same level. In the middle of 1997, the Asian crisis occurred which resulted in significant writing down of holdings in Asian currencies. The crisis, which had an impact on the global economy, did not result in a major drop of the average price of the banks in the sample. There can be a multitude of reasons for this, such as the implementation of effective hedging strategies or having relatively small holdings in the currencies affected. On the other hand, this was also the period of the Dot.com bubble which started to slowly build up from 1995 onwards. This may explain why the Asian crisis did not result in a price decline, but instead resulted in prices stabilising over the next two years. Prices subsequently rose until during 2001 the Dot.com bubble burst. From 2001 onwards, prices kept on declining until 2004, then increased again towards 2007 and declined again. Given the severity of the current financial crisis, the years 2001 – 2008 do not appear to accurately reflect the actual developments in the market.

One of the disadvantages of using average per share prices is that mergers, stock splits and the issue of additional shares result in a declining share price which is unrelated to market movements. In addition, average price per share data is distorted by banks that have a high share price and a low number of shares. In order to provide a view on the development of the global markets, the total estimated fundamental value and total price provides a fuller picture of the developments.

In order to achieve this, both the price per share and the estimated fundamental value per share are multiplied by the number of shares and added up to provide a total for the sample of 115 banks.

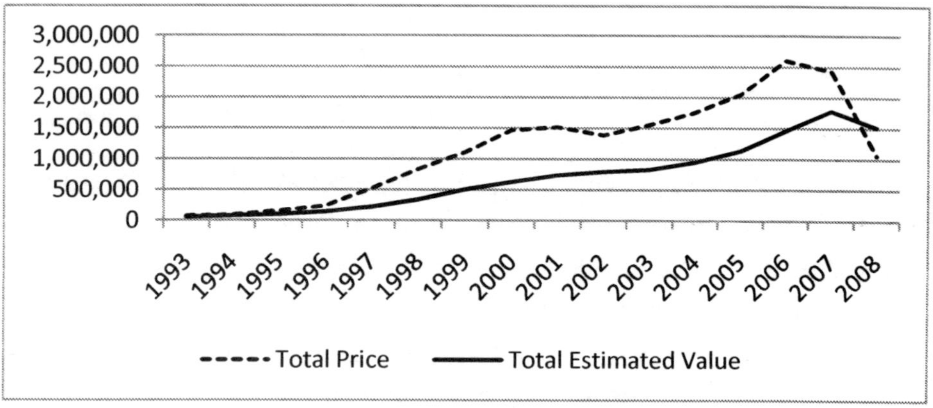

Figure 5 – Total price and total estimated fundamental value 1993 – 2008 (in $mn)

Figure 5 shows that the impact of the combined Asian crisis and Dot.com bubble results in a relatively flat price movement from 2000 – 2001 with a slight reduction in 2002. The total estimated fundamental value does not appear to be impacted, and continues to gradually increase over the period, a development that continued through to

2007 when the price fell slightly followed by the rapid decline at the start of the current financial crisis.

Compared to previous years, 2008 is the first time the total price is below the total estimated fundamental value. This is likely due to the uncertainty surrounding the extent of the occurrences and the lack of information on how individual banks were affected by the sub-prime crisis. As a result of this in combination with the additional capital and major write-downs announced, shareholders were actively selling in a market where demand had as good as disappeared. As can be observed from figure 5, analysts have also reduced their forward expectations resulting in a lower total estimated value.

Not all banks in the sample are affected in the same way. During the sample period, and particularly during the last year, the number of American banks has reduced to a larger extent than the European banks. In part this is due to increased M&A activity over the period. In addition, many have recently been closed by their respective state's Department of Financial Institutions. This process typically involves appointing the Federal Deposit Insurance Corporation (FDIC) as a receiver whose first priority is to find a bank that takes on the responsibility for all deposits. As a result of these developments, however, the geographical distribution of the banks has changed as represented in figure 6.

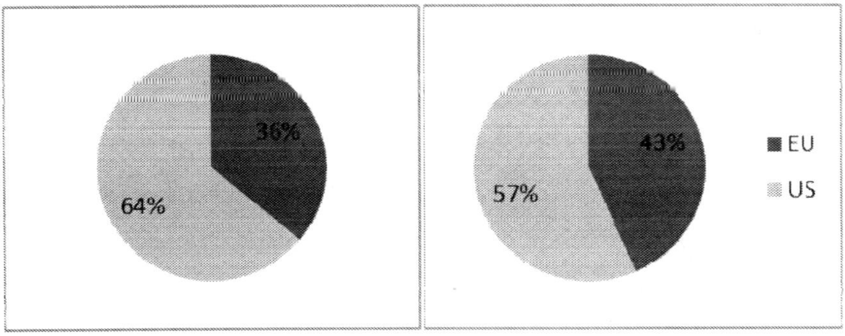

Figure 6 Geographical distribution of the original (left) and final (right) sample

Looking at the two main geographical areas individually, it becomes clear that different areas have responded to the financial crisis in different ways.

The United States

Compared to the total sample as represented in figure 5, the data for the United States represented in figure 7 below, shows that the average total price for the 65 US banks in the sample is generally further away from the estimated fundamental value. In addition reactions to the various crises in the earlier periods appear to be more pronounced, such as the price reduction at the end of the dot.com boom.

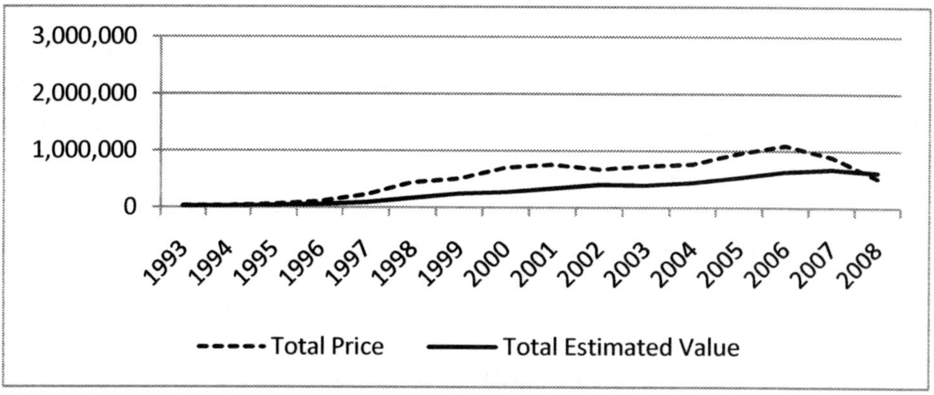

Figure 7 –Total price and total estimated fundamental value in the US 1993 – 2008 (in $mn)

In addition, prices seem to decline rapidly from 2006 onwards, without first showing signs of stabilisation, and do not drop as far below the estimated fundamental value as the overall banks in the sample.

The European Union

Banks in the European Union have seemingly suffered less from the dot.com boom as can be seen in the data of the remaining 50 European-based banks represented in figure 8. For the European banks, the price generally seems to move closer to the estimated fundamental value, but the drop in 2007 appears to be more severe than for the American banks. Towards the end of 2006, the potential write-offs associated with the subprime mortgage market are starting to become clear, but are at that point in time still thought to be largely restricted to the American market. As a result, the price of European banks still showed a marginal increase compared to 2005. As the full impact on European banks started to become clear, the prices began to fall significantly.

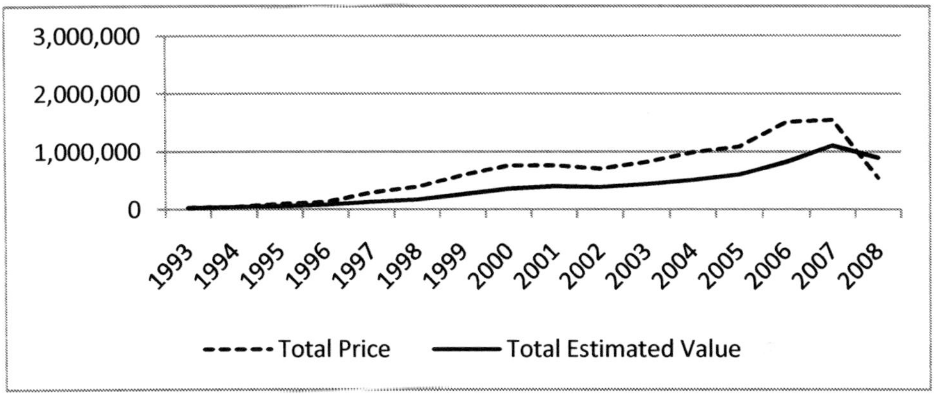

Figure 8 –Total price and total estimated fundamental value in the EU 1993 – 2008 (in $mn)

Equally, the estimated fundamental value has declined, but to a larger extent than the estimated fundamental value for the American banks in the sample.

Reasons for different behaviour of prices per region

There could be a number of reasons for the differences in the development of price and estimated fundamental value between the United States and Europe, and they are difficult to establish while the credit crisis is still developing. However, some of the reasons could include:

- *Market emotions*. Investors, faced with substantial uncertainty over the value of their investments, may have experienced panic and sold in large quantities disregarding fundamental values. Excess supply and a relative lack of demand resulted in significant price reductions.

- *Efficient Hedges*. Some of the banks in the sample may have implemented more efficient hedges than others. Some of the banks that received funds from the US Government under the Troubled Asset Relief Program (TARP) have openly admitted that their hedges on the demise of Lehman's and AIG generously off-set the losses incurred.
- *Size of Exposure*. Some of the banks in the sample will have had little or no exposure to any of the assets underlying the various asset bubbles.
- *Effectiveness of government measures*. Particularly in the current credit crisis, the effectiveness of the combined government measures including the nationalisation of banks and measures to motivate spending and investments will play an important role in the development of price and fundamental value.
- *Timing*. At the start of the current credit crisis, the expectation was that the problems with subprime mortgages were restricted to the United States and did not impact any other jurisdiction. As time passed, however, it became clear that the financial system is truly global and many other banks had also incurred large losses as a result of their exposure to derivative products based on these mortgages.

8 Concluding Remarks

This book has two distinct parts. Part 1 details how the fundamental value of conventional and Islamic banks can be estimated using a Residual Income based valuation model, with Part 2 exploring additional items such as behavioural finance, the impact of news and media, Value at Risk and the possibility to predict asset bubbles.

8.1 The Model and Parameters

The Residual Income model applied is not new, but based on the model that is extensively tested for non-financial firms and fine-tuned by Frankel and Lee.

The findings for conventional banks are based on panel data analysis using which shows that as long as the parameters of the model are estimated correctly, the estimated fundamental value explains a large percentage of cross-sectional variations in market prices. The parameters are determined as follows:

- *Earnings* is measured using Earned for Ordinary;
- *Capital* consists of share capital and reserves but excludes any deposits given to the bank since these are considered to be of an operational nature;
- *Risk* is measured by β and used to determine the required return on equity;
- *Growth* is based on the I/B/E/S consensus forecast; and
- *Book value* is represented by the reported book value.

The analysis was carried out using two samples, one to estimate the regression, and one control sample. Both samples contained an equal number of banks with the same ratio of US versus European banks and a similar population size. The results show a high correlation between the market price and the value estimated using the Residual Income model, controlled for first-degree serial autocorrelation and heteroskedasticity. The goodness of fit for the estimation sample is 80%, with a confidence level of 99%. The control sample is then used to measure how close the unrestricted estimates of the control sample come to the coefficient found in the estimation sample.

The results from the various analyses imply that more than 80% of the cross-sectional variation in stock prices can be explained by the estimated fundamental value calculated using the Residual Income Model, which is in line with the findings of Frankel and Lee who use the same model for non-financial industries. Based on the results of this study it can be concluded that the Residual Income model can be applied to banks, and it is established that there is a relationship between the accounting measure and the stock market measure. A significant percentage of the cross-sectional variations in stock market prices of conventional banks can be explained by the value of the firm calculated by the model.

The Islamic financial industry is young, but is growing rapidly. Historically Islamic and conventional banks are based on the same core principle, which is to provide financial intermediation between holders of surplus funds and those requiring funds for investment. Apart from the fact that Islamic finance operates based on the principles of the Sharia'a, which prohibits, among others, interest and speculation, the main difference between the Islamic and conventional banking industry is related to the further development of the industries. Where the first conventional banks started in the 17th century, Islamic banks only started operating in their current form in 1975. As a result of the fact that the Islamic banking industry is still relatively young, a number of issues related to availability and transparency of data still occur. Moreover, Islamic banks predominantly operate in countries where the capital market is not fully developed, so that share prices for such banks are either not determined in an efficient market setting or not available at all.

The study presented in this book has found that it is in principle possible to apply the Residual Income model to Islamic banks, although a number of issues will need to be resolved before more definite conclusions can be drawn. Non-availability of market data, restricted sample size, the need to use proxies, and the lack of transparency of accounting information all need to be taken into consideration. However, the economic principles of Islamic and conventional banks are similar, and no indication has been found that the logic of the Residual Income model cannot be applied to Islamic banks. Support for the validation of the results can be found in the comparison of the average value created by Islamic banks and conventional banks, which shows a similar trend, although especially in earlier years the results for Islamic banks are more volatile than the ones for conventional banks. The findings are indicative of the possibility of applying the Residual Income model to determine the value of Islamic banks, as well as the potential to apply the model such that comparisons can be made with conventional banks once the issues found are resolved.

8.2 Capturing Bank Fundamental Value

In a semi-strong form efficient market, it is assumed that all publicly available information is immediately and fully reflected in the share price. Any profits from seeking out over- or undervalued stocks will only be available to investors with insider information. However, as the test results illustrate, it is possible to identify over- or under-valuation of a set of firms in an industry without access to insider information. The Residual Income model used to estimate fundamental value is after all solely using publicly available information.

Over the past 15 years, the financial system has experienced a variety of booms and busts, some more severe than others. In each case, share prices have responded more strongly than the estimated fundamental values. The most recent financial crisis has caused more disturbance, however, than the previous Asian crisis and Dot.com boom. This becomes clear from the difference in the panel data test results.

Period	Price explained by value
1993 – 2002	80.6%
1993 – 2008	78.5%

Table 9 – Proportion of price explained by fundamental value

During the first period, 1993 – 2002, in excess of 80% of the price was explained by the estimated fundamental value of the banks. In the period 1993 – 2008 this was reduced by more than 2%. Most of this difference can be ascribed to the development of prices during the period 2006 – 2008. The end of the current crisis is not yet in sight though, and only time will tell whether the results represented in table 9 above might be distorted only temporarily.

Other factors, such as herd behaviour, have been identified as potential contributors to the remaining 20% of banking sector share prices.

A brief look at the FTSE All Shares Index shows that, although the reactions of the index to economic crises appear much more severe than in the bank sample, the trend line is very similar across other sectors of the economy, as can be seen from figure 9 below.

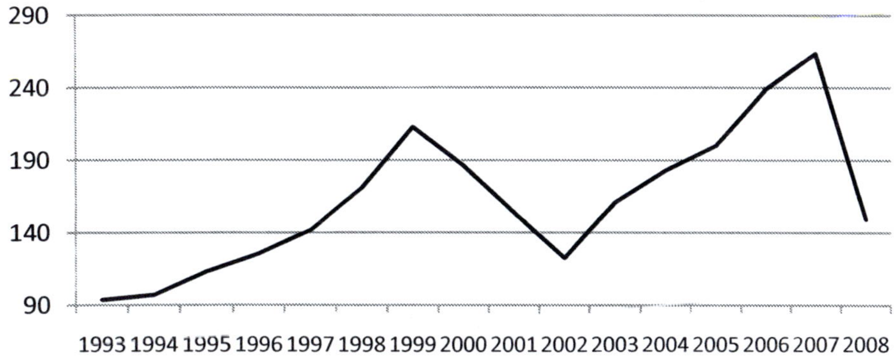

Figure 9 – FTSE All Share Index 1993 - 2008

Determining the estimated fundamental value for the constituents of the index is well beyond the remit of this book, but the above illustrates how connected the global economy appears to be.

In uncertain times the goodness of fit of the Residual Income model used to estimate the fundamental value of the banks in the sample deteriorates slightly. However, the model identified is this study and described in detail in Chapter 2 generally holds up well, even in uncertain times. At the aggregated sample level, the estimated fundamental value can be used as a check to determine whether the share prices are inflated or depressed.

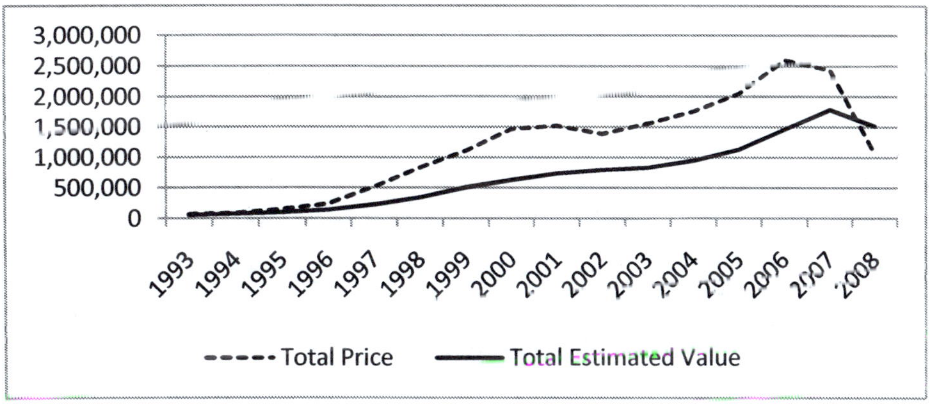

Figure 10 – Total price and total estimated fundamental value 1993 – 2008 (in $mn)

As illustrated by figure 10 above, the spread between the estimated fundamental value and price widens and contracts over time. The fundamental value does however capture a significant part of the total price. It is not until 2008 that we see a significant adjustment of the price which is likely not solely caused by the estimated fundamental value but in part a consequence of the way investors have responded to the significant events that took place during the later period of the study. It is unfortunately too early to determine whether this might have been an overreaction.

The results for individual banks differ and are dependent on individual circumstances at the end of each period that is measured. Careful analysis of the individual banks gives an indication that that the fundamental value estimated using the Residual Income model may enable the investor to seek out over- and undervalued banks. From the sample of 115 banks used for this research, a few interesting observations can however be made:

- The general trend shows that, like the average, individual banks are generally overvalued, in some times quite significantly;
- Although there are exceptions, the US based banks tend to follow each other more closely than the European banks;
- A relatively higher proportion of European banks appears undervalued in the years 2003 and 2004, which could indicate that these banks have generally suffered more from the Asian crisis and the Dot.com boom;
- Individual banks' market capitalisation is generally higher than the estimated fundamental value, and can occasionally be as much as seven times as high as the estimated fundamental value. Very few occasions of under-valuation are observed, although during the earlier period of the study one bank's market capitalisation was 25% of estimated fundamental value, and during the period 2003 – 2004,

two of the banks market capitalisation was as low as 80% of estimated fundamental value. Banks are generally overvalued, and rarely undervalued. This likely occurs due to the perceived "safety" of bank shares.

- The highest relative overvaluation achieved by a UK based bank was 3.5 times the estimated fundamental value. This number may be misleading due to the fact that part of the purchase price was paid in shares and part in cash.

Other interesting points can be found when analysing the individual banks, but extensive further research will however be required to determine the validity of the statements made here.

Glossary

Term	Definition
AAOIFI	Accounting and Auditing Organisation for Islamic Financial Institutions
APT	Arbitrage Pricing Theory
β	Beta – systematic, undiversifiable risk of an investment in comparison with the overall market
B^e_t	Book value of a firm per share at time *t*
CAPM	Capital Asset Pricing Model
CDO	Collateralised Debt Obligation
CML	Capital Market Line
CV	Continuing Value
DCF	Discounted Cash Flow
EPS	Earnings per Share
E-V	Expected Return - Variance
EVA	Economic Value Added
F1MN	I/B/E/S consensus growth forecast, 1 year forward
F2MN	I/B/E/S consensus growth forecast, 2 years forward
FCF	Free Cash Flow
g	Long-term sustainable growth rate
I/B/E/S	International Brokers' Estimated System. Collection of estimates for over 45,000 companies provided by 1,200 contributors
IAS	International Accounting Standard
Ijara	Bilateral contract allowing the transfer of the usufruct. Lease.
IRR	Investment Risk Reserve
Istisna	Sale with deferred delivery. Payment can be in a lump sum in advance or progressively in accordance with progress made. Delivery of good is deferred

Term	Definition
LIBOR	London Interbank Offer Rate
LTCM	Long Term Capital Management
LTMN	I/B/E/S consensus long-term growth expectation
Mudaraba	Partnership contract. Sub-set of Musharaka
Mudarib	Party in a *mudaraba* contract providing knowledge and skill
Musharaka	Deferred payment sale or instalment credit sale
OLS	Ordinary Least Squares
PER	Profit Equalisation Reserve
Qard	Interest free loan
R^2	Goodness of Fit
Rab al Mal	Investor
RAROC	Risk Adjusted Return on Capital
r_e	Required return on equity
R_f	Risk free rate of return
RI	Residual Income
RIA	Restricted Investment Account. The bank is bound by the contract with the customer which specifies how the funds can be applied. No capital guarantee
Riba	Interest
R_m	Market rate of return
ROE	Return On Equity
Salam	Sale with deferred delivery. Payment is paid in full and up front, delivery of good is deferred
SEC	Securities and Exchange Committee (US)
Sharia'a	Ethical framework of Islam, often referred to as Islamic Law
SML	Security Market Line
URIA	Unrestricted Investment Account. The bank applies the funds to their day-to-day business. No capital guarantee
VaR	Value at Risk

Term	Definition
V^e_t	Fundamental per share value of a firm estimated using a Residual Income Model at time *t*
WACC	Weighted Average Cost of Capital
X	Independent variable in the regression model
Y	Dependent variable in the regression model
Zakat	Obligatory donation to charity for those who can afford it. 2.5% of wealth when based on a lunar calendar year, 2.5775% for a solar calendar year.

Bibliography

AAOIFI (2002) *Accounting, Auditing and Governance Standards for Islamic Financial Institutions*, Accounting and Auditing Organisation for Islamic Financial Institutions, Bahrain: AAOIFI

Al-Deehani, T., R.A.A. Karim and V. Murinde (1999) *The Capital Structure of Islamic Banks under the Contractual Obligation of Profit Sharing,* International Journal of Theoretical and Applied Finance, 2(3), 243-283

Al-Saddah, A.K.I (2000) *Regulation of Financial Reporting by Islamic Banks*, Mphil Thesis, Guildford: University of Surrey

Archer, S., and R.A.A. Karim (2001) *On Capital Structure, Risk Sharing and Capital Adequacy in Islamic Banks,* ABACUS, under review

Armstrong, J.S. (2001) *Principles of Forecasting: A Handbook for Researchers and Practitioners,* Den Haag: Kluwer Academic Publishers

Bahrain Stock Exchange (1998) *Factbook 1998,* Manama: Bahrain Stock Exchange

Bahrain Stock Exchange (2004) *Monthly Closing Prices 2002* [online], Manama: Bahrain Stock Exchange website (www.bahrainstock.com)

Banz, R.W. (1981) *The Relationship Between Returns and Market Value of Common Stocks,* Journal of Financial Economics, 9(1), 3-18

Barker, R. (2001) *Determining Value – Valuation Models and Financial Statements,* Harlow: Pearson Education Limited

Barry, C.B., J.W. Peavy III and M. Rodriguez (1997) *Emerging Stock Markets: Risk, Return and Performance,* Charlottesville: The Research Foundation of The Institute of Chartered Financial Analysts

Basu, S. (1983) *The Relationship Between Earnings' Yield, Market Value and Return for NYSE Common Stock,* Journal of Financial Economics, 12, 129-156

Berkowitz, M.K. (1990) *Estimating the Market Risk for Nontraded Securities: An Application to Canadian Public Utilities,* International Review of Financial Analysis, 7(2), 171-179

Bernstein, Peter L. (1998) *Against the Gods: The Remarkable Story of Risk New York,* John Wiley & Sons

Bernstein, R and C. Pigler (1997/1998) *An Analysis of EVA Part I and II* Quantative Viewpoint, No. 19 - December 1997 and No. 20 - February 1998, Merrill Lynch

Bhandari, L.C. (1988) *Debt/Equity Ratio and Expected Common Stock Returns: Empirical Evidence,* The Journal of Finance, 43(2), 507-528

BIBLIOGRAPHY

Biddle, G.C., R.M. Bowen and J.S. Wallace (1997) *Does EVA beat earnings? Evidence on associations with stock returns and firm values*, Journal of Accounting and Economics, 24(11), 301-336

Biddle, G.C., R.M. Bowen and J.S. Wallace (1998) *Economic Value Added: Some Empirical EVAdence*, Managerial Finance, 24 (11), 60-71

Black, F. (1972) *Capital Market Equilibrium with Restricted Borrowing,* Journal of Business, 45, 444-455

Black, F. (1980) *The Magic in Earnings, Economic Earnings versus Accounting Earnings,* Financial Analysts Journal, 36(November/December), 19-24

Black, F., M.C. Jensen and M. Scholes (1972) *The Capital Asset Pricing Model: Some Empirical Tests,* Studies in the Theory of Capital Markets, M.C. Jensen ed. New York: Praeger Publishers

Bolt, W. and A.F. Tieman (2002) *When Basle II Does Not Work: Contingency Rules Versus Fixed Requirements,* De Nederlandsche Bank Research Department, Research Memorandum WO no. 681, Amsterdam: DNB

Bolt, W. and A.F. Tieman (2004) *Banking Competition, Risk, and Regulation,* IMF Working Paper WP/04/11, Washington: IMF

Bookstaber, R. (1999) *Risk Management in Complex Organizations*, Financial Analysts Journal, 54(2), 18-20

Boyd, J.H. and M. Gertler (1994) *Are Banks Dead? Or, Are the Reports Greatly Exaggerated?,* Conference Proceedings; The (declining?) Role of Banking; The 30th Annual Conference on Bank Structure and Competition; Chicago: Federal Reserve Bank of Chicago, 85-117

Brealey, R.A., S.C. Myers and A.J. Marcus (2003) *Fundamentals of Corporate Finance*, International Edition, New York: McGraw-Hill

Breeden, D.T. (1979) *An Intertemporal Asset Pricing Model with Stochastic Consumption and Investment Opportunities,* Journal of Financial Economics, 7, 265-296

Brendon, P (2009) *With Bubbles, it's plus ça change…,* Financial World, July/August 2009, London: CSFI

Bruner, R.F., R.M. Conroy, E. Li, E.F. O'Halloran and M.P. Lleras (2003) *Investing in Emerging Markets.* Charlottesville: The Research Foundation of AIMR

Centre for the Study of Financial Innovation (2009) *Grumpy Old Bankers: Wisdom from Crisis Past*. London: CSFI

Çizakça, M. (1996) *A Comparative Evolution of Business Partnerships – The Islamic World and Europe, with Specific Reference to the Ottoman Archives*, Leiden: E.J. Brill

Clubb, C. (2002) *On the equivalence of Cash Flow and Residual Income Approaches to Equity Valuation*, Presented at the European Accounting Association Annual Congress, Copenhagen, April 2002

Conover, C.M., G.R. Jensen and R.R. Johnson (2002) *Emerging Markets: When Are They Worth It?* Financial Analysts Journal, 58(2), 86-95

Constantinides, G.M., Harris, M, Stulz, R.M (2003), *Handbook of the Economics of Finance: Corporate Finance*, Amsterdam: Elsevier B.V.

Copeland, T.E, T. Koller and J. Murrin (2000) *Valuation: Measuring and Managing the Value of Companies,* 3rd Edition, New York: John Wiley & Sons

Copeland, T.E and J.F. Weston (1992) *Financial Theory and Corporate Policy* Third Edition, New York: Addison Wesley Publishing Company

Cox, J.C., J.E. Ingersoll Jr. and S.A. Ross (1985) *An Intertemporal General Equilibrium Model of Asset Prices,* Econometrica, 53(2), 363-384

Easton, P.D. (1985) *Accounting Earnings and Security Valuation: Empirical Evidence of the Fundamental Links*, Journal of Accounting Research, 23(Supplement), 54-77

Faff, R.W., R.D. Brooks and H.Y. Kee (2002) *New Evidence on the Impact of Financial Leverage on Beta Risk: A Time-series Approach,* North American Journal of Economics and Finance, 13(1), 1-20

Fairfield, P (1994) *P/E, P/B and the Present Value of Future Dividends*, Financial Analysts Journal, 49(4), 23-31

Fama, E.F. (1970) *Efficient Capital Markets: A Review of Theory and Empirical Work,* The Journal of Finance, 25(2), 383-417

Fama, E.F. (1991) *Efficient Capital Markets: II,* The Journal of Finance, 46(5), 1575-1617

Fama, E.F. and K.R. French (1992) *The Cross-Section of Expected Stock Returns,* The Journal of Finance, 47(2), 427-465

Fama, E.F. and K.R. French (1997) *Industry Costs of Equity,* Journal of Financial Economics, 43, 153-193

Fama, E.F. and K.R. French (2000) *Forecasting Profitability and Earnings,* Journal of Business, 73(2), 161-175

Fama, E.F. and J.D. MacBeth, (1973) *Risk, Return and Equilibrium: Empirical Tests,* Journal of Political Economy, 81(3), 607-636

Feltham, G. and J.A. Ohlson (1995) *Valuation and Clean Surplus Accounting for Operating and Financial Activities*, Contemporary Accounting Research, 11(2),

689-731

Feltham, G. and J.A. Ohlson (1999) *Residual Earnings with Risk and Stochastic Interest Rates*, The Accounting Review, 74(2), 165-183

Fernandez, P. (2001) *Company Valuation Methods. The Most Common Errors in Valuation*, IESE Business School, Working Paper June 26 2001

Frankel, R. and M.C. Lee (1998) *Accounting Valuation, Market Expectation, and Cross-sectional Stock Returns*, Journal of Accounting and Economics, 25, 283-319

Gujarati, D.N. (2002) *Basic Econometrics*, 4th Edition, New York: McGraw-Hill International Editions

Heffernan, S. (1996) *Modern Banking in Theory and Practice,* Chichester: John Wiley & Sons Ltd.

Higgins, R.C (1998) *Analysis for Financial Management,* Columbus: Irwin

Hirtle, B. (1991) *Factors Affecting the Competitiveness of Internationally Active Financial Institutions* FRBNY Quarterly Review Spring 1991, New York: Federal Reserve Bank of New York, 38-51

Hsiao, C. (2003) *The Analysis of Panel Data,* 2nd Edition, Cambridge: Cambridge University Press

Jacobs, B. and K. Levy (1988) *On the Value of 'Value'* , Financial Analysts Journal, 44(4), 47-62

Jensen, M.C. (1978) *Some Anomalous Evidence Regarding Market Efficiency,* Journal of Financial Economics, 6, 95-101

Jorion, P. (2001) *Value, Risk and Control: a Dynamic Process in Need of Integration*, Mastering Risk – Volume 1: Concepts, Editor: James Pickford, Harlow: Pearson Education Ltd., 119-124

Jorion, P. (2006) *Value at Risk. The New Benchmark for Managing Financial Risk*. New York: McGraw Hill

Kaplan, R.S. and D.P. Norton (1992) *The Balanced Scorecard – Measures that Drive Performance*, Boston: Harvard Business Review, January – February, 71 - 79

Kimball, R.C. (1997) *Innovations in Performance Measurement in Banking*, Boston: New England Economic Review, May/June, 23-38

Kimball, R.C. (1998) *Economic Profit and Performance Measurement in Banking,* Boston: New England Economic Review, July/August, 35-53

Lee, C.M.C., J. Myers and B. Swaminathan (1999) *What is the Intrinsic Value of the Dow,* The Journal of Finance, 54(5), 1693-1741

Lintner, J. (1965) *The Valuation of Risky Assets and the Selection of Risky Investments in Stock Portfolios and Capital Budgets*, Review of Economics and Statistics,

47(1), 13-37

Lundholm, R.J. and T.B. O'Keefe (2001) *Reconciling Value Estimates from the Discounted Cash Flow Model and the Residual Income Model*, Contemporary Accounting Research, 18(2), 311-335

Lundholm, R.J. and T.B. O'Keefe (2001a) *On Comparing Residual Income and Discounted Cashflow Models of Equity Valuation: A Response to Penman*, Contemporary Accounting Research, 18(4), 693-696

Markowitz, H. (1952) *Portfolio Selection*, The Journal of Finance, 12(1), 77-91

Marshall, A. (1895) *Principles of Economics*, 3rd Edition, London: Macmillan & Co

Marston, F and S. Perry (1996) *Implied Penalties for Financial Leverage: Theory versus Empirical Evidence,* Quarterly Journal of Business and Economics, 35(2), 77-97

McKenzie, M.D., R.D. Brooks, R.W. Faff and Y.K. Ho (2000) *Exploring the Economic Rationale of Extremes in GARCH generated Betas. The Case of US Banks,* The Quarterly Review of Economics and Finance, 40, 85-106

Merton, R.C. (1973) *An Intertemporal Capital Asset Pricing Model,* Econometrica, 41(5), 867-887

Merton, R.C. and A.F. Perold (1993) *Theory of Risk Capital in Financial Firms*, Journal of Applied Corporate Finance, 6(3), 16-33

Miller, M. H. and Modigliani, F. (1961). *Dividend Policy, Growth and the Valuation of Shares*. Journal of Business, 34, 411-33.

Mossin, J. (1966) *Equilibrium in a Capital Asset Market,* Econometrica, 34(4), 768-783

Myers, J.N. (1999) *Implementing Residual Income Valuation with Linear Information Dynamics*, The Accounting Review, 74(1), 1-28

Nienhaus (2001) *Transparency, Governance and Risk Management In Islamic Financial Institutions: Roles of Stakeholders In Islamic Financial Institutions,* Paper presented to the conference Transparency, Governance and Risk Management in Islamic Financial Institutions, Beirut

O'Farrell, J. (2008) in *An Utterly Impartial History of Britain: or 2000 years of Upper Class Idiots in Charge*, London: Black Swan

Ohlson, J.A. (1990) *A Synthesis of Security Valuation Theory and the Role of Dividends, Cash flows and Earnings,* Contemporary Accounting Research, 6(2-II), 648-676

Ohlson, J.A. (1995) *Earnings, Book Values, and Dividends in Equity Valuation,* Contemporary Accounting Research, 11(2), 661-687

Peasnell, K.V. (1982) *Some Formal Connections Between Economic Values and Yields and Accounting Numbers*, Journal of Business Finance & Accounting, 9(3), 361-381

Penman, S.H. (1992) *Return to Fundamentals,* Journal of Accounting, Auditing and Finance, 7, 465-483

Penman, S.H. (1996) *The Articulation of Price-Earnings Ratios and Market-to-Book Ratios and the Evaluation of Growth*, Journal of Accounting Research, 34(2), 235-259

Penman, S.H. (1998) *A Synthesis of Equity Valuation Techniques and the Terminal Value Calculation for the Dividend Discount Model,* Review of Accounting Studies, 2, 303-323

Penman, S.H. (2001) *On Comparing Cash Flow and Accrual Accounting Models for Use in Equity Valuation: A Response to Lundholm & O'Keefe,* Contemporary Accounting Research, 18(4), 681-692

Penman, S.H. and T. Sougiannis (1998) *A Comparison of Dividend, Cashflow and Earnings approaches to equity valuation*, Contemporary Accounting Research, 15(1), 343-382

Peterson, P.P. and D.R. Peterson (1996) *Company Performance and measures of Value Added,* Charlottesville: The Research Foundation of The Institute of Chartered Financial Analysts

Porter, M.E. (1980) *Competitive Strategy* New York: Free Press

Roache, Shaun K. and Rossi, M (2009) *The Effects of Economic News on Commodity Prices: Is Gold Just Another Commodity?* IMF Working paper 09/140, Washington: IMF

Roll, R. (1977); *A Critique of the Asset Pricing Theory's Tests – Part I: On Past and Potential Testability of the Theory*, Journal of Financial Economics, 4, 129-176

Rosly, S.A and M.A.A Bakar (2003), *Performance of Islamic and Mainstream Banks in Malaysia*, International Journal of Social Economics, 30(12), 1249-1265

Ross, S.A. (1976) *The Arbitrage Theory of Capital Asset Pricing,* Journal of Economic Theory, 13, 341-360

Saudi Arabian Monetary Agency (2004) *Tables of Annual Report, Share Market Statistics* [online], Riyadh: www.sama.gov.sa, publications and statistics, tables of annual report

Schiller, R.J. (2005) *Irrational Exuberance* second edition, Princeton, New Jersey: Princeton University Press

Schoon, N (2008) *Islamic Banking and Finance*, London: Spiramus Press

Sharpe, W.F. (1964) *Capital Asset Prices: A Theory of Market Equilibrium under*

Conditions of Risk, The Journal of Finance, 19(3), 425-442

Shefrin, H (2002) *Beyond Greed and Fear: Understanding Behavioral Finance and the Psychology of Investing.* Oxford: Oxford University Press

Simon, Herbert (1957). *Models of Man, Social and Rational: Mathematical Essays on Rational Human Behavior in a Social Setting*. New York: Wiley.

Sloan, R.G. (1996) *Using Earnings and Free Cash Flow to Evaluate Corporate Performance*, Journal of Applied Corporate Finance, 9(1)

Smith, A. (1881) *An Inquiry into the Nature and Causes of the Wealth of Nations, Abridged version with notes and appendices by Wolsely P. Emerton, M.A. B.C.L.*, Oxford: James Thornton

Solomons, D. (1965) *Divisional Performance: Management and Control*, Columbus: Irwin

Standard & Poor's (2002) *Classic Ratings Approach Applied to Islamic Banks despite Industry Specifics*, London: 27 November 2002

Stark, A.W. (1997) *Linear Information Dynamics, Dividend Irrelevance, Corporate Valuation and the Clean Surplus Relationship*, Accounting and Business Research, 27(3), 219-228

Stewart, G.B. III (1990) *The Quest for Value*, New York: Harper Business Press

Sundararajan, V. and L. Errico (2002) *Islamic Financial Institutions and Products in the Global Financial System: Key Issues in Risk Management and Challenges Ahead*, IMF Working Paper WP/02/192, Washington: IMF

Talib, N.N. (2007) *The Black Swan – The Impact of the Highly Improbable* London: Penguin Books

Thomas, J.J. (1983) *An Introduction to Statistical Analysis for Economists*, London: London School of Economics Handbooks in Economic Analysis, Second edition

Tomkins, C. and R.A.A. Karim (1987) *The Shari'ah and its Implications for Islamic Financial Analysis: An Opportunity to Study Interactions Among Society, Organisation, and Accounting*, The American Journal of Islamic Social Sciences, 4(1), 101-115

Vogel, F.E. and Hayes III, S.L. (1998) *Islamic Law and Finance – Religion, Risk, and Return*, Den Haag: Kluwer Law International

Walker, M. (1997) *Clean Surplus Accounting Models and Market-based Accounting Research: A Review*, Accounting and Business Research, 27(4), 341-355

Walker, M. and P. Wang (2001) *Towards an Understanding of Profitability Analysis within the Residual Income Valuation Framework*, Manchester: Manchester University and Middlesex University, Unpublished paper September 2001

BIBLIOGRAPHY

Watson, C.J., P. Billingsley, D.J. Croft and D.V. Huntsberger (1993) *Statistics for Management and Economics,* Massachusetts: Allyn and Bacon, Fifth Edition

Index

INDEX